BMW ISETTA

FACTORY REPAIR

MANUAL

VelocePress would like to thank BMW A.G. for their permission to reprint this work.

ISBN 1 58850 036 5
This work was previously published in 1957 by BMW A.G., Munich as publication number MC 123.

© 2002 TheValueGuide, Inc., Reno, Nevada 89509

All Rights Reserved. This work may not be reproduced or transmitted in any form without the express written consent of the publisher.

Trademarks used herein are for identification only.

Information on the Use of this Publication

As a service to the Isetta enthusiast who wishes to better understand the workings of their automobile, VelocePress is proud to present the 1957 BMW Isetta Factory Manual. Condensed from its original four-language format, the material presented is unchanged from the last edition and has not been updated to reflect changes in common practice, availability of materials or increased awareness of chemical toxicity. As such it is advised that the user consult with an experienced professional prior to undertaking any procedure described herein.

Contents

TRANSPORTATION FOR ISETTA	9
SPECIAL TOOLS FOR BMW ISETTA	13
TECHNICAL DATA OF THE MOTOCOUPE BMW ISETTA	17
GROUP M ENGINE	23
GROUP G TRANSMISSION	67
GROUP H REAR AXLE	77
GROUP V FRONT SUSPENSION	91

ANNEX FOR EXPORT MODEL 1957

GROUP V FRONT SUSPENSION CONTINUED	103
GROUP L STEERING	117
GROUP F SPRINGS AND SHOCK ABSORBERS	129
GROUP B BRAKES, WHEELS, TIRES	139
GROUP A BODY	149
GROUP R CHASSIS FRAME	161
GROUP E ELECTRICAL SYSTEM	167
GROUP W MAINTENANCE	199

TRANSPORTATION FOR ISETTA

Isetta Factory Repair Manual

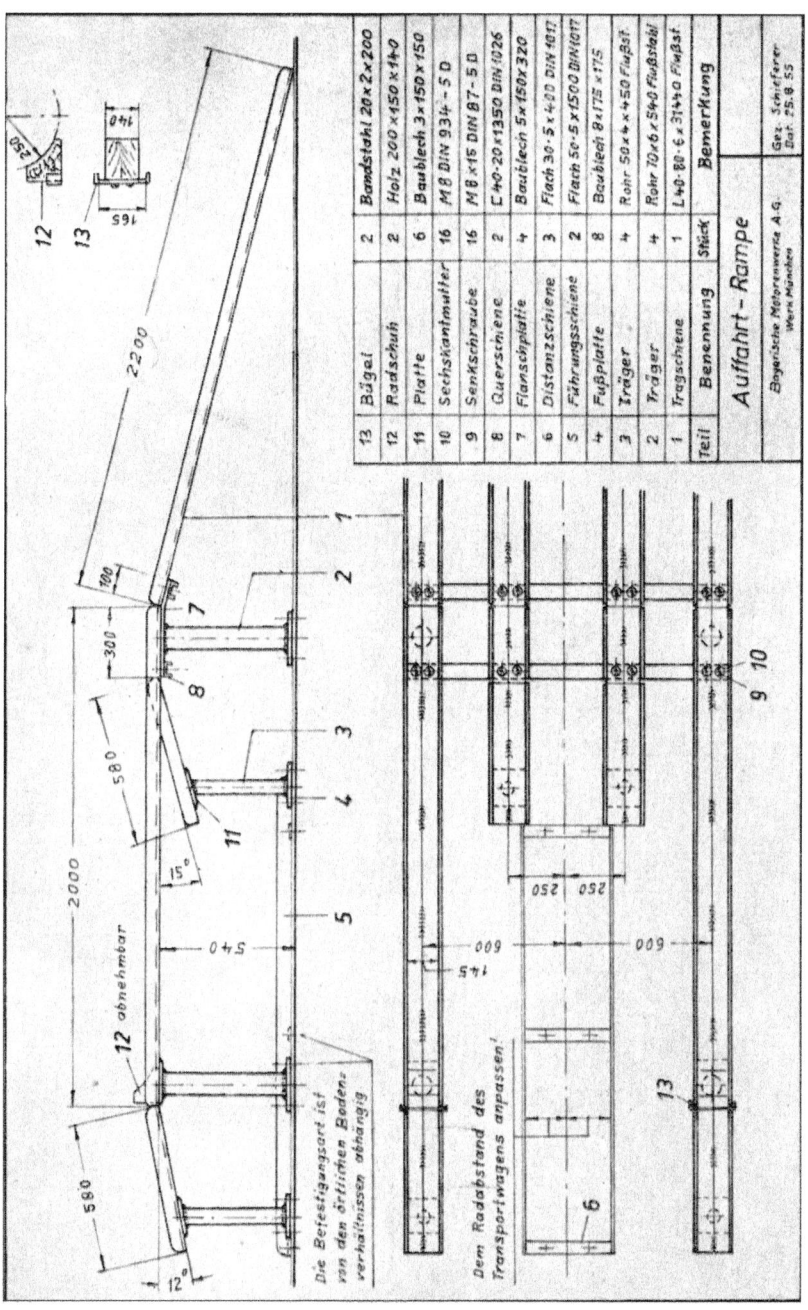

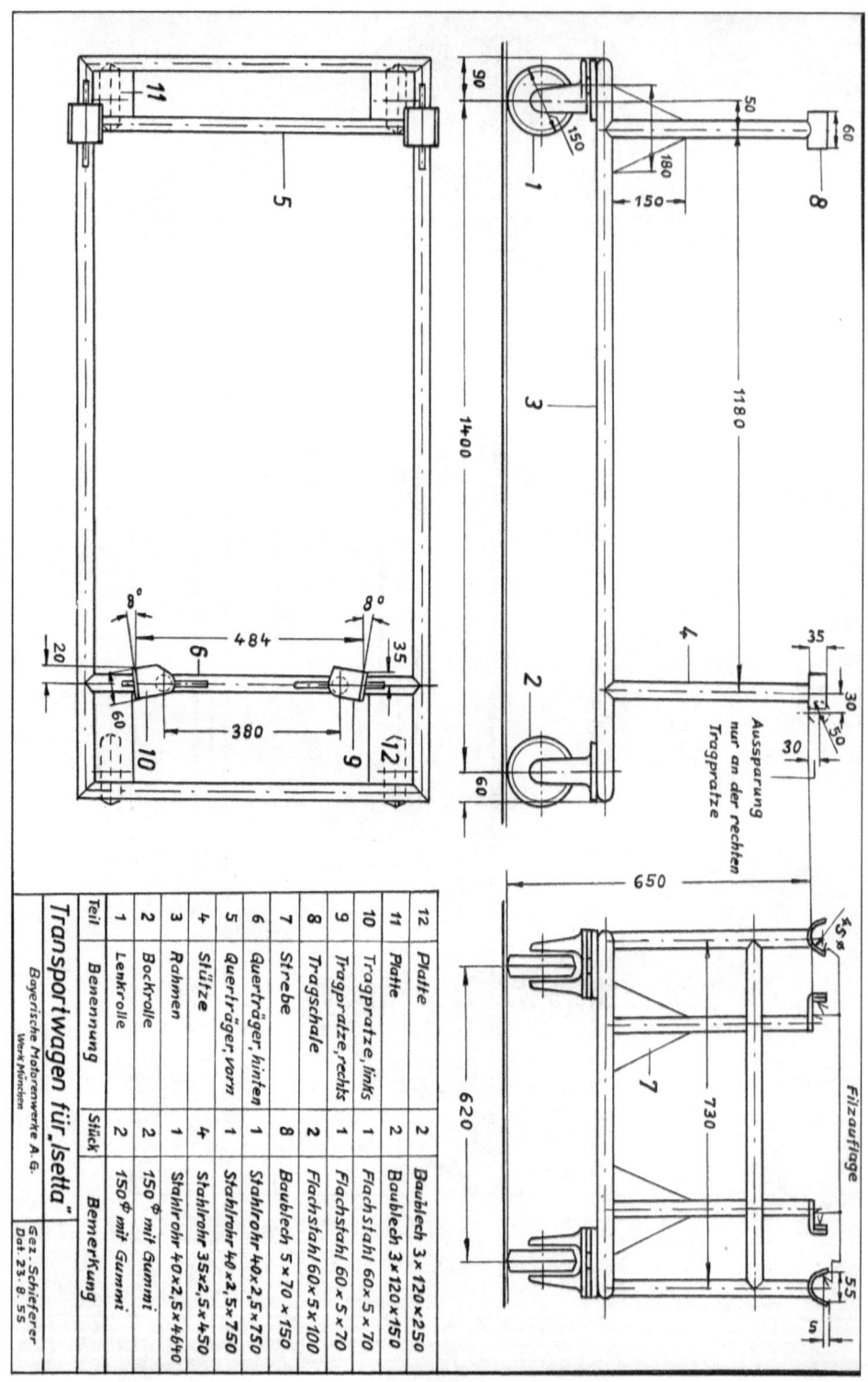

SPECIAL TOOLS
FOR
BMW ISETTA

Special Tools for BMW Isetta

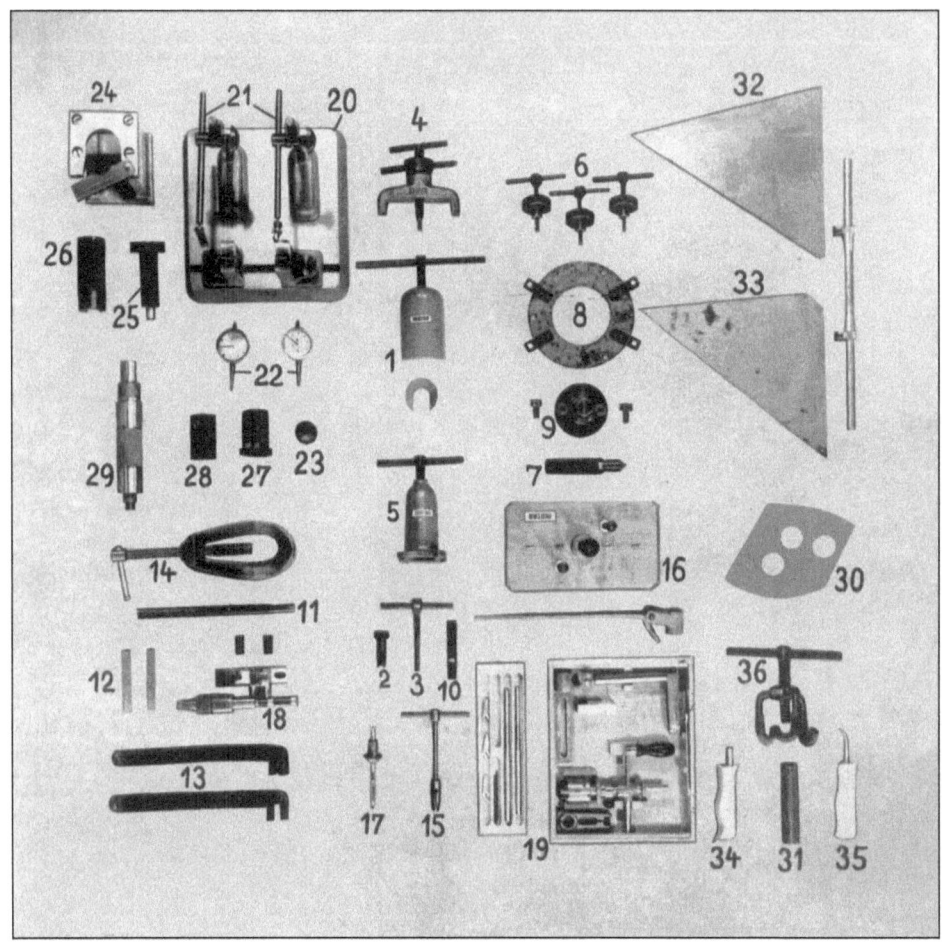

1.	M 299a	Puller, ball bearing (with modification)(Matra device)
2.	M 527	Puller screw, blower wheel (Matra tool)
3.	M 528	Puller spindle, dynamo starter armature (Matra tool)
4.	M 355a	Puller, camshaft (Matra tool)
5.	M 467	Puller, bearing cover plate (Matra tool)
6.	M 357 a	Clamping screws for clutch installation (Matra device)
7.	M 529	Arbour for centering of clutch (Matra tool)
8.	M 498	Locking fixture for flywheel (Matra device)
9.	M 311	Puller, flywheel, with two sets of screws (Matra device)
10.	M 530	Arbour for adapting protection tubes of rocker arm push rods (Matra tool)
11.	W 5002	Drift punch, gudgeon pin (to be made in the dealer's shop=shop-made tool)
12.	L 5036	Parallels for alignment of connecting rods (Shop-made tool)
13.	W 5021	Straightening tool, connecting rod (Shop-made tool)
14.		Puller, gudgeon pin (commercial type)
15.	M 368	Holder, for grinding-in valves with 7 mm stem diameter (Matra tool)
16.	M 361 a	Holding board for intake and exhaust valves and valve spring lifter (Matra Device)
17.		Valve guide reamer (commercial type)

18.		Reaming tool, connecting rod bushing (commercial type)
19.		Valve seat and valve face turning tool (commercial type)

No.: 17, 18, 19 to be supplied by
Messrs. Ludwig Hunger,
Werkzeugfabrik
Munchen-Grobhadern
Grafelfinger Strabe 146

23.	M 531	Compensating bushing for checking true rotation of crankshaft in conjunction with device M 353 A-C (Matra device)
29.	V 5046	Lapping tool for connecting rods (shop-made tool) (Caution: Notice modification of drawing)
30.		Gauge for entering transmission shafts (shop-made tools)
32.		Gauge for checking castor 12° (shop-made tool)
33.		Gauge for checking king pin inclination 5° (shop-made tool)
34.		Special tool for inserting weatherstrip retainers (commercial type) Order No.: 36 943
35.		Special tool for installation of glass panels (commercial type) No.: 36 941

No. 34 and 35 made by
Messrs. Happich G.m.b.H.
Wuppertal-Elberfeld.

36.		Puller, steering wheel

For the gauges 32 and 33 see drawings under Section R Chassis frame.

TECHNICAL DATA
OF THE
MOTOCOUPE BMW ISETTA

Engine

Make and type – BMW Isetta 250 cc or 300 cc
Cycle – Fourstroke Otto
Number of cylinders and arrangement – 1 cylinder with blower cooling
Valves – Overhead, in V-arrangement
Camshaft drive – Roller chain
Valve operation – Tappets, pushrods and rocker arms

	250 cc engine	300 cc engine
Bore	68mm(2.67in.)	72mm(2.83in.)
Stroke	68mm	73mm
Piston displacement	247 cc	295 cc
	(15.07 cu. in.)	(18.61 cu. in.)
Compression ratio	6.8 to 1	6.8 to 1
Power	12 bhp at 5800 rpm	13 bhp at 5200 rpm

Medium piston speed – 13.3 m/sec. = 43.6 ft./sec. At n=5800 rpm
Valve clearance (with engine cold)
      Intake = 0.15 mm (.006 in.)
      Exhaust = 0.20 mm (.008 in.)
Lubricating system – Force feed lubrication
Oil pump – Gear-type oil pump
Oil capacity, engine – 3.1 Imp. pints = 3.6 U.S. pints
Lubricant – Trade-mark HD oil SAE 20 in winter; SAE 40 in summer

Carburetor

	250 cc	300 cc
Model "Bing"	1/22/97	1/22/98

Adjustment

Passage	22mm=86in.	22mm
Main jet	130	130
Needle jet	1310/6	1308
Jet needle	2023	2023
Idling jet	35	35
Starter jet	55	55
Needle position	1	2
Weight of float	7 grams	7 grams-.25 oz.
Pilot air screw opened	1 to 2 turns	1 to 2 turns

Fuel supply - by gravity
Air cleaner – Micronic filtering element in air silencer

Clutch
Single plate dry clutch

Transmission
BMW four forward speed and reverse gearbox

	1st	2nd	3rd	4th	Reverse
Gear ratios	10.05	5.17	3.54	2.70	12.15
Overall gear ratios	23.21	12.15	8.17	6.23 30.0	

Oil capacity, transmission - .96 Imp pints = 1.1 U.S. pints (trade-mark oil SAE 40)

Final drive
Type – Short rigid axle driven by chain in oil-bath case forming unit with the axle housing
Power transmission – through transverse resilient mounted drive shaft and totally enclosed, fully adjustable chain drive in oil bath.
Final drive ratio – 2.31:1 (30/13 teeth)
Overall gear ratio in 4th gear – $I = i_1 \cdot 1_0 = 2, 70 . 2, 31 = 6, 25:1$

Chassis frame
Trapeze form
Type – Rigid tubular chassis frame

Steering
Type – steering screw and nut
Steering gear ratio – 16:1
Turning circle diameter – approx. 8 m (24 feet)

Suspensions
Front – Independent (swing arm damped by coil spring and friction-type shock absorber)
Rear – Two quarter-elliptic leaf springs and telescopic shock absorbers

Wheels and tires
Type of wheels – steel disc wheels with split rims to facilitate tire mounting
Rims – 3, 00 D-10
Tires – Five times, overdimension size 4.80x10"
Tire pressure, front 17 lbs./sq.in.; rear 14 lbs./sq.in.
Camber – 1 1/2°
King pin inclination - 5°

Toe-in – 4 to 5 mm - .16 to .20", measured on the rim borders, front and rear
Castor - 12°

Brakes
Type – Hydraulic (BMW-Teves)
Footbrake operates on all four wheels
Hand brake operates on the rear wheels
Brake design – Internal shoe brakes, (floating)
Brake drum diameter – 7 in.
Total brake lining area – 49.9 sq. in.

Fuel tank
Capacity – 2.8 Imp. Gal. = 3.4 U.S. gal. With reserve fuel supply of 65 Imp. Gal. = .8 U.S. gal.

Electrical system – 12 volts
Battery – 12 volts/24 ampere hours
Dynamo (generator) starter – 12 volts/130 watts (combined)

Designation
Dynamo starter Noris LA 12/130 R
Regulator type – Voltage regulator (F) RS/A 12/130 combined with starter relay
Starting RPM – approx. 1,200
Rated continuous output – 130 watts at 1,800 RPM
Drive ratio – 1:1
Starter operation combined with ignition switch

Ignition
Battery-ignition 12 volts
Ignition timing – automatic, with governor control on blower wheel
Initial ignition timing - 7° before T.D.C. at idling speed
Maximum advance - 7°+35°=42° before T.D.C.
Contact breaker – Breaker gap 0.4 mm = .016 in.
Sparking plug – Bosch W 240 T1 (electrode gap 0.6 mm = .024 in.)

Electric horn – Noris HE 12

Radio unit (optional item)
Installation intended for medium-waves wireless sets only.

Main dimensions

Track (tread), front – 47.2 in.
Track (tread), rear – 20.4 in.
Wheelbase – 58 in.
Overall dimensions
Length – 89.9 in.
Width – 54.3 in.
Height (unladen) – 52.6 in.

Weight

Kerb weight – approx. 770 lbs.
Carrying capacity – 507 lbs.

Road performance

	250 cc engine	300 cc engine
Maximum speed	53 mpg	56 mph
Climbing ability – First gear 1 in 3		

Running-in speeds for the first 1,200 miles

Miles registered on speedometer:

Miles per hour in (gear)	1st	2nd	3rd	4th
0 to 600 not over	10	18.5	31	40
600 to 1200	Increased speeds for short distances			
over 1200	15	30	40	53 (56 with 300 cc engine)

GROUP M
ENGINE

M1 Removing and refitting engine

Fig. 1

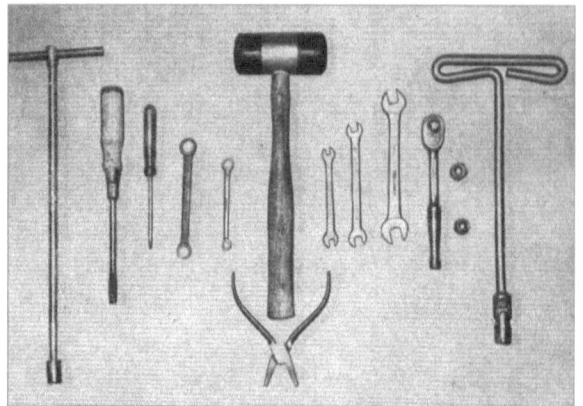

Tools: Wheel nut spanner, screwdriver, electrical screwdriver, socket spanners 10/12/14 mm with universal joint, 12-point ring spanner 10/14 mm, open ended spanners 7/11/14 mm, ratchet wrench, plastic mallet, flat pliers.

Fig. 2

1. Turn off the petrol tap, remove seat and backrest.

2. Disconnect the negative lead from the body. (socket spanner 10mm)

3. Disconnect the wires from the cable connector group. (blue, green and black-brown)(electrical screwdriver)

Fig. 3

4. Remove wheel cover plates from rear wheels and slacken wheel nuts. (screwdriver, wheel nut spanner)

5. Support the vehicle on the rear.

6. Remove the two rear wheels. (wheel nut spanner)

7. Remove engine covering panel and detach starter. (open ended spanner 7 mm)

8. Detach ignition coil and withdraw high-tension cable. (socket spanner 10 mm)

9. Draw the three disconnected wires (job 3) outwards.

10. Remove the two mudguards (fenders). (socket spanner 10 mm)

Fig. 4

11. Detach petrol pipe from carburetor.

12. Remove clamp securing the hose connection toward the air silencer. (flat pliers)

Fig. 5

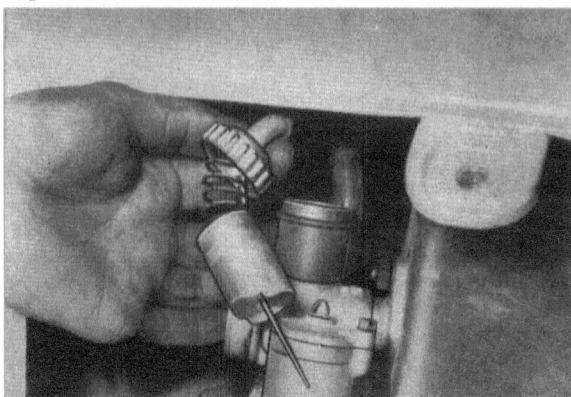

13. Unscrew carburetor cover assembly, withdraw throttle slide and envelop it in a cloth.

Fig. 6

14. Remove carburetor starter slide (choke piston) and wrap it in a clean cloth. (open ended spanner 11 mm)

15. Detach exhaust flange from engine. (socket spanner with universal joint 12 mm)

16. Disconnect the silencer from its rear attachment.
(socket spanner 10 mm with ratchet, ring spanner 10 mm for counteracting on unscrewing)

Fig. 7

17. Slacken the two upper rubber mountings on carrier and clutch flange. (socket spanner 14 mm with universal joint, ring spanner 14 mm, open ended spanner 14 mm)

Isetta Factory Repair Manual

Caution: When refitting the two upper rubber mountings after joining engine and transmission, engage them first on the gearbox flange and then on the engine carrier. Before connecting the earth (ground) lead polish the contact spots.

18. Remove the lower pair of the four screws fixing gearbox to engine. (ring spanner 14 mm)

Fig. 8

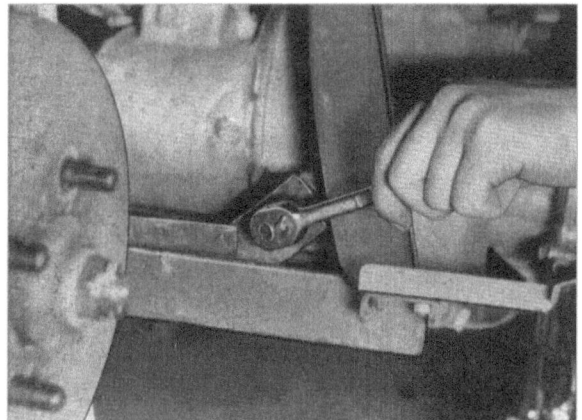

19. Slacken the two lower rubber mountings, right and left. (socket spanner 14 mm with ratchet)

Fig. 9

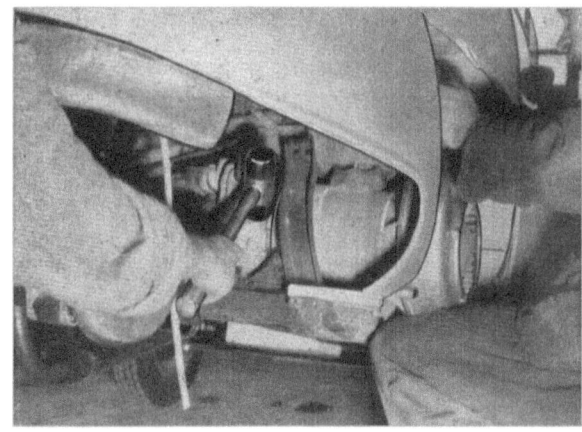

20. Support the engine on the knees for removal, remove the two rubber mountings and applying slight taps with a plastic mallet withdraw engine from transmission. Down transmission to the frame.

27

Fig. 10

Caution: When refitting lift transmission correspondingly and engage engine on the four gearbox fixing screws.

The refitting is carried out in precisely the reverse order.

M2 Removing and refitting engine with transmission
(The body is removed)

Fig. 11

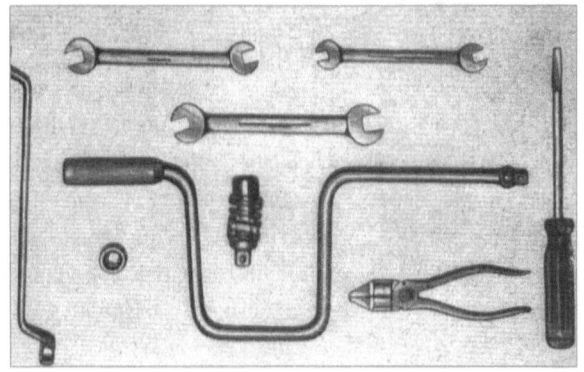

Tools: open ended spanners 10/12/14 mm, socket spanner 14 mm with universal joint, ring spanner 14/17 mm, screwdriver 6 mm, pliers for cotter pins.

Fig. 12

1. Slacken clamp securing exhaust tube beneath the silencer, push exhaust tube rearwards. (open ended spanner 10 mm)

Fig. 13

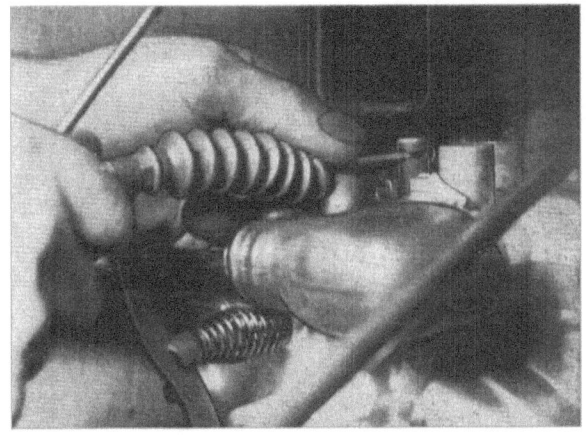

2. Remove cotter pin on both gear selector rods on transmission, remove bolts and take off selector rods. (cotter pin pliers)

3. Slacken locknut for clutch adjustment, turn adjusting nut fully in, press clutch level on and unhook the Bowden wire. (open ended spanner 12 mm)

Fig. 14

4. Adjust clutch, unscrew nut fully out of the lever, remove pressure spring on clutch lever.

5. Remove throttle slide from carburetor.

Fig. 15

Caution: Wrap throttle slide in a clean cloth and tie it up on the frame by means of an insulating tape. Put a clean cloth in the carburetor.

6. Remove air duct rubber elbow from carburetor by loosening the securing clamp. (screwdriver 6 mm)

Fig. 16

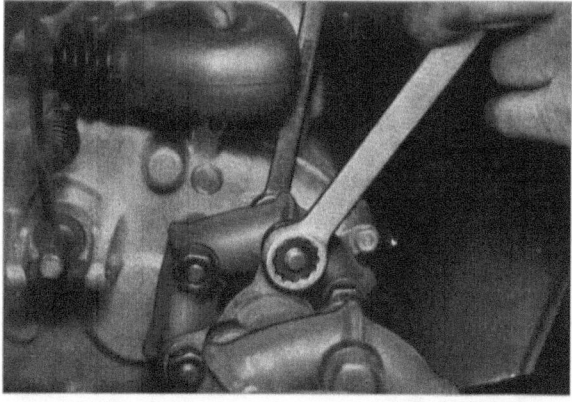

7. Detach silencer from engine. Three nuts on cylinder head, two nuts on top and bottom of transmission. (socket spanner with universal joint 14 mm)

8. Remove nuts from three bolts on the universal joint at gearbox end. (ring spanner 17 mm and open ended spanner 17 mm for counteracting on unscrewing)

Attention: These three bolts must be removed that secure the rubber ring to the three-arm drive flange on gearbox shaft.

Fig. 17

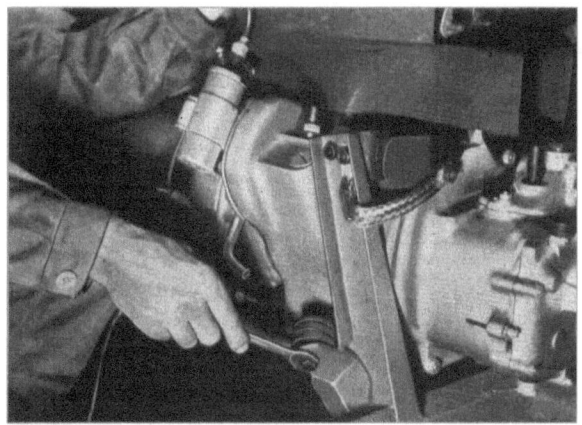

9. Remove the two lower engine fixing screws on the rubber mountings, right and left. (open ended spanner 14 mm)

Fig. 18

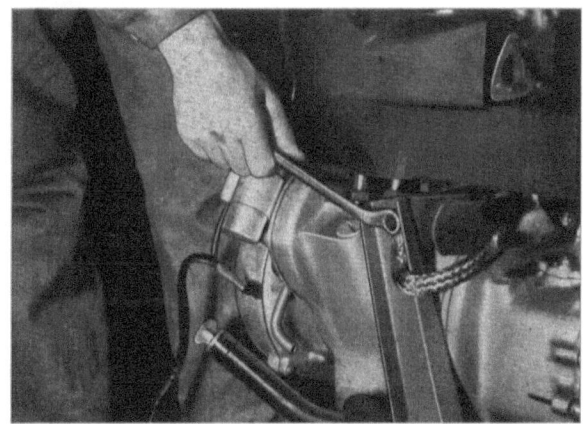

10. Slacken the four upper engine fixing screws at right and lift. (ring spanner 14 mm)

Fig. 19

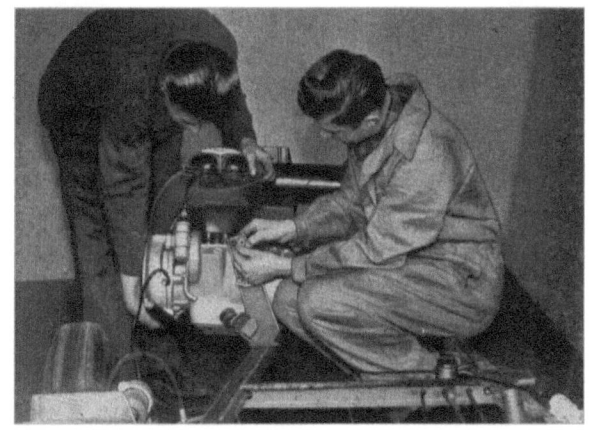

<u>Attention</u>: One screw will be left on either side and not removed completely unless the assistant holds the engine for removal. On refitting don't forget the earth (ground) lead. Polish the contact surface.

11. Raise engine, remove the fixing screws from the upper carrier and withdraw the engine from the universal joint.

Fig. 20

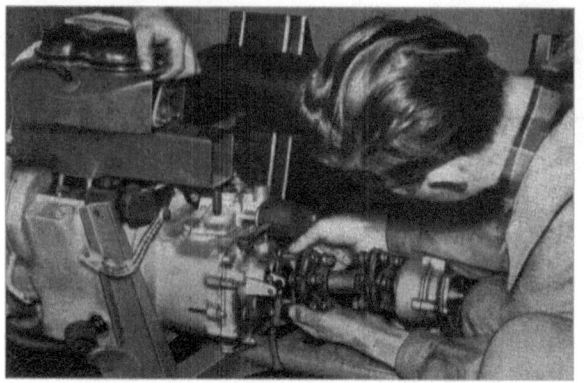

Attention: When installing engine have it raised by an assistant and enter the tree bolts on the universal joint.

Then only screw in the two lower engine fixing screws on the rubber mountings and thereafter the four upper engine holding screws. The further refitting is carried out in reverse order to that indicated for removal.

M3 Removing and refitting clutch
(Engine is removed following M1 or M2)

Fig. 21

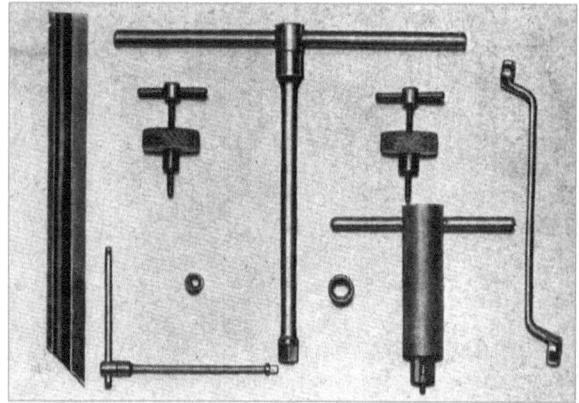

Tools: Socket spanners 10 and 14 mm, ring spanner 14 mm, two clamping screws for clutch, No. 357, centering arbour for clutch, No. 529.

Isetta Factory Repair Manual

Fig. 22

1. Detach gearbox from engine housing. (4 nuts with socket spanner 14 mm and ring spanner 14 mm)

Caution: The two upper engine fixing screws must not be slackened.

Fig. 23

2. Remove clutch unit. (socket spanner 10 mm)

Caution: To release clutch unit and to compress it on refitting use two clamping screws for clutch reassembly Matra 357 from the tool set for motorcycles.

Caution: For refitting clutch unit employ clutch centering arbour No. 529.

Fig. 24

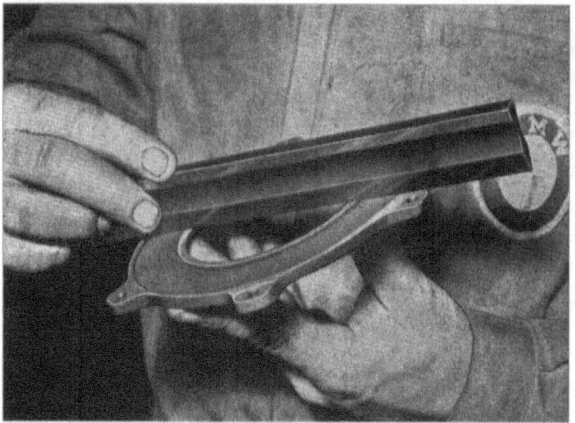

3. With the aid of a straight-edge check driven disc and pressure plates for distortion.

Fig. 25

Caution: If the clutch disc is worn or the pressure plates warped (blue coloured) replace the parts in question.

Caution: On reassembly of clutch make certain that the protruding part of driven disc hub shows outwards. The plain (unchambered) face of clutch pressure plate must press against the driven disc. Position of clutch parts.

The reassembly is carried out in precisely the reverse order.

M4 Readjusting clutch
M6 Basic adjustment of clutch

Fig. 26

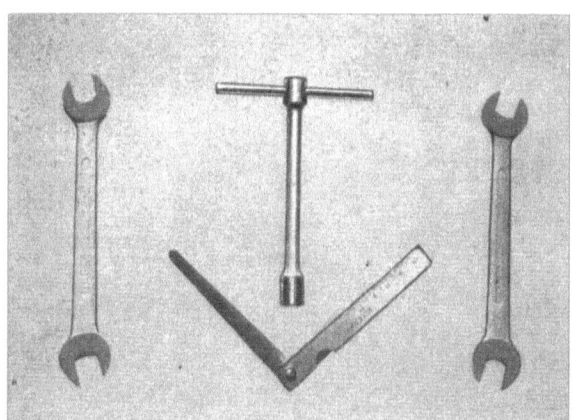

Tools: Two open ended spanners 12 mm, socket spanner 10 mm, feeler gauge 0.2 mm (.008")

M4 Readjusting the clutch (in vehicle)

Fig. 27

1. Slacken locknut of clutch adjusting screw (Two open ended spanners 12 mm)

2. Unscrew clutch adjusting screw out of the clutch lever until the free movement at the clutch pedal pad is about 15 mm (.6 in.)l. (Clearance between clutch actuating screw and clutch rod about 0.2 mm = .008 in.)

M6 Basic adjustment of clutch
(engine and transmission are refitted upon the frame)

Fig. 28

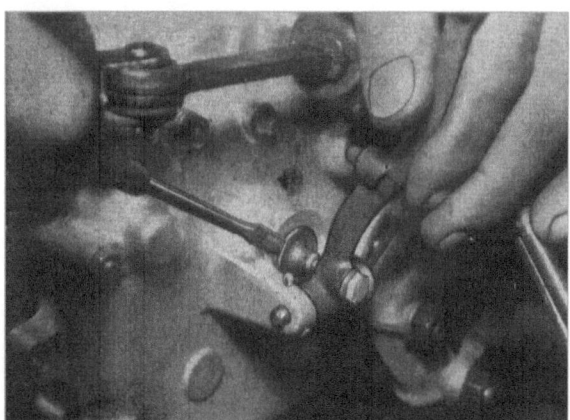

1. Adjust the clutch adjusting screw so that the clutch rod flushes with the surrounding plain cast portion of transmission case.

Fig. 29

2. If this position cannot be reached with the adjuster, alter the shims behind the adjusting screw until the thrust unit of clutch actuating mechanism flushes correctly. (socket spanner 10 mm)

Fig. 30

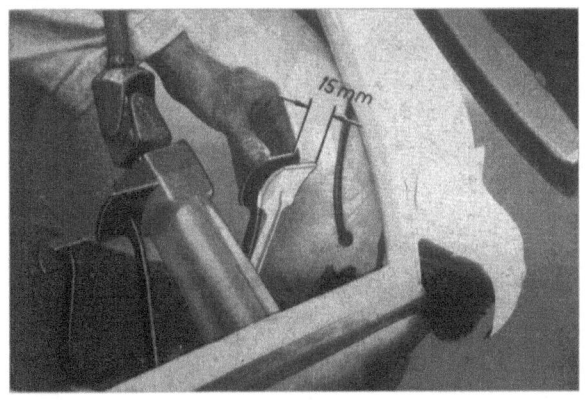

3. Adjustment of pedal clearance as per M4. (two open ended spanners 12 mm)

Caution: The clutch being correctly adjusted and the adjusting screw completely screwed-in the clearance between the thrust unit and the clutch actuating screw must be 0.2 mm = .008 in. and the free movement at the clutch pedal pad about 15 mm = .6 in.

M9 Dismantling and reassembling engine

Fig. 31

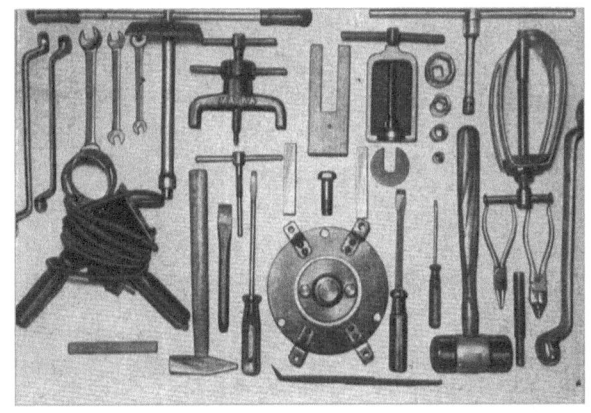

Tools: Open ended spanners 9 and 14 mm, ring spanners 19 and 27 mm, socket spanners 14/17/36 and 10 mm, screwdrivers 6/8 and 10 mm, torque spanner, hammer, chisel, pointed pliers, wooden piece, plastic mallet, flywheel fixture No. 498, puller screw for blower wheel No. 527, puller screw for armature No. 528, puller No. 299 with compensating ring No. 299a, piston board, heating sleeve for piston, gudgeon pin drift No. 5002, gudgeon pin puller, camshaft puller No. 355, flywheel puller No. 311.

Fig. 32

1. Fit engine open support stand. (open ended spanner 14 mm)

2. Drain engine oil (ring spanner 19 mm)

3. Disconnect ignition coil connections from terminals 1 and 15. (open ended spanner 9 mm)

4. Remove ignition coil with holding bracket. (socket spanner 10 mm)

Fig. 33

5. Remove carburetor. (open ended spanner 14 mm)

6. Remove rocker covers. (open ended spanner 14 mm)

7. Remove the baffle assemblies of air cooling arrangement

    a) three slotted head screws, front

    b) two slotted head screws bottom

    c) one slotted head screw, rear top (screwdriver 6 mm)

8. Remove cap covering the dynamo-starter assembly. (screwdriver 6 mm)

9. Remove blower housing, four slotted head screws. (screwdriver 8 mm)

10. Apply flywheel fixture No. 498. (open ended spanner 10 mm)

Fig. 34

11. Remove blower wheel fixing screw. (socket spanner 17 mm)

12. Remove blower wheel with the aid of screw-type puller No. 527.

Fig. 35

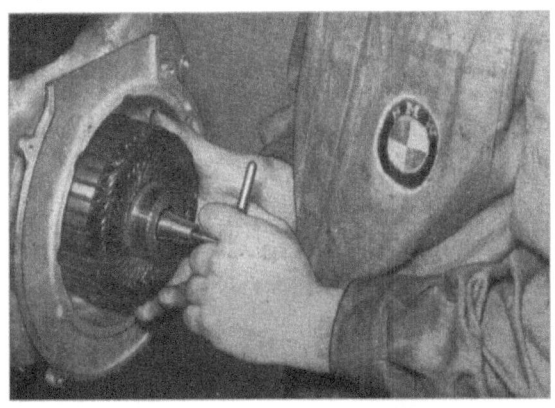

13. Remove frame and field coil assembly of dynamo-starter unit, four slotted head screws (screwdriver 8 mm)

Caution: When assembling the generator and starter unit release the carbon brushes from spring pressure by withdrawing the springs and push brushes back to avoid damaging them.

14. Remove armature with the aid of screw-type puller No. 528.

Fig. 36

15. Remove spring washer from crankshaft journal. (screwdriver 6mm)

16. Unscrew nuts and screws securing camshaft drive covering unit.

3 screws 10 mm
6 nuts 10 mm
1 countersunk screw

(open ended spanner and socket spanner 10 mm, screwdriver 8 mm)

Caution: Don't forget the countersink screw on right-hand border of housing

Fig. 37

17. Remove timing cover by tapping it off with the aid of a wooden tool

Caution: The wooden tool must not be applied on the front flange of housing, but on the base of this unit (Figure 37). At the opposite side apply tool upon the rib between flange and base of the casting. Never try to enter a screwdriver between the castings. If the housing is too tight to tap it apart, heat it slightly.

Isetta Factory Repair Manual

Fig. 38

18. Withdraw ball bearing from crankshaft. (Puller No. 299 with compensating ring No. 299a)

Caution: When removing with compensating ring and refitting with tube piece grasp ball bearing inner race only. Before refitting heat ball bearing on a heating plat up to about 60° C = 140° F.

19. Remove rotary valve on breather unit.

Fig. 39

20. Open chain lock.

Caution: When refitting chain make sure that the closed end of chain lock cotter regards in direction of chain rotation, so that the camshaft sprocket turns in a clockwise direction.

Fig. 40

21. Unscrew cylinder head holding down screws (4 thorough screws carrying the rocker assemblies) and remove cylinder head. (socket spanner 14mm)

Caution: When assembling tighten cylinder head with the aid of a torque spanner to 3.5 mkg = 25.3 ft. lbs. Tighten screws evenly in a diagonal order.

Assembling the engine
(Fitting chain and adjusting camshaft drive)

1. Set the piston on T.D.C.

Caution: To replace timing chain without engine removal set engine on T.D.C. through the inspection hole machined in engine crankcase. The arrow engraved in flywheel must register with the dash on housing.

Fig. 41

2. Rotate camshaft to its overlap dead center position. A straight-edge placed upon the pushrods must be parallel to the joint face of cylinder head.

Fig. 42

Caution: When refitting chain without engine removal apply a punch mark. The third tooth of camshaft sprocket, counted from the drill hole for the driven peg to the left, must shown vertically downwards.

Fig. 43

3. Return camshaft sprocket and engage chain on top.

Fig. 44

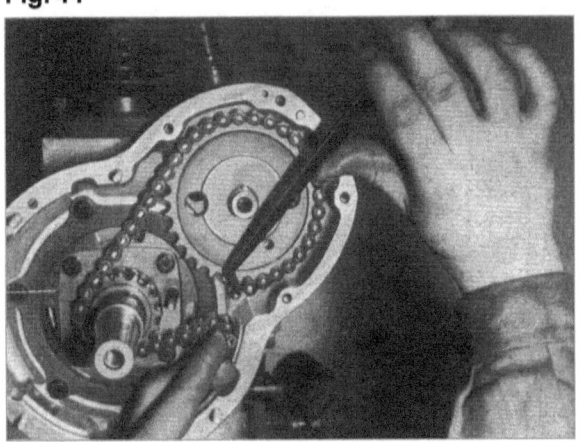

4. Rotate camshaft sprocket to the right and engage chain upon crankshaft sprocket in the punch marked position (T.D.C. position).

Fig. 45

5. With the aid of an appropriated tool bring chain members together and push the free chain member upon the lock member.

6. Place chain lock in position.

7. Fit chain lock cotter with the closed end in direction of rotation.

Caution: To compensate chain tension there are provided three different lengths and colours marks for identification purposes: Blue = short chain, red = middle chain, green = long chain. The fitted chain must not show more than 3 mm (.12") of play (slack) when applying thumb pressure. Fit chain of corresponding length with the colour mark outward.

Further dismantling

Fig. 46

22. Withdraw push rods.

23. Slacken cylinder base clamping nuts. (open ended spanner 14 mm)

24. Insert piston board.

25. Remove gudgeon pin retaining circlip. (pointed pliers)

26. Heat piston with heating sleeve up to about 60° C = 140° F and press out gudgeon pin (electric heating sleeve, gudgeon pin drift).

Fig. 47

Caution: If the piston pin does not come out by thumb pressure, do not tap, but apply piston pin remover device.

Fig. 48

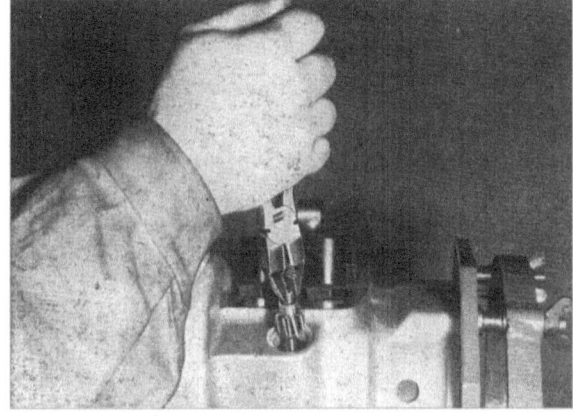

Caution: Always assemble pistons and pins bearing the same colour marks for identification purposes. When assembling piston heat same upon heating plate or in oil up to 60° C = 140° F and warm gudgeon pin slightly.

27. Remove tappets.

Caution: Identify the tappets by tags so that they can be correctly reinstalled in the same position and location.

28. Unscrew plug giving access to the oil pump drive.

29. Remove oil pump drive.

Fig. 49

30. Enter screwdriver through the two holes in camshaft sprocket in order to remove the two screws fixing the camshaft bearing holding bush. (screwdriver 10 mm)

31. Remove camshaft with the aid of camshaft puller No. 355.

<u>Caution</u>: Handle camshaft carefully to prevent it from hurts.

Fig. 50

<u>Caution</u>: When refitting make certain that the camshaft sprocket aligns with the crankshaft sprocket so that the timing chain runs correctly. Eliminate an eventual misalignment by pressing camshaft sprocket a bit more inwards.

32. Remove two screws from crankshaft front bearing cover plate. (socket spanner 10 mm)

33. Remove crankshaft sprocket. (puller No. 299)

<u>Caution</u>: To refit the sprocket heat it to about 150° C = 300° F, tilt engine and slide sprocket on vertically standing shaft downwards.

34. Detach oil sump. (socket spanner 10 mm)

35. Remove oil pump, straighten bent ears of lock washer and remove two screws. (hammer, chisel, socket spanner 10 mm)

36. Straighten locking lugs on flywheel nut lock washer. (hammer, chisel)

Caution: When refitting bend lock washer slightly before installation to facilitate completion of bending on the fitted washer.

Fig. 51

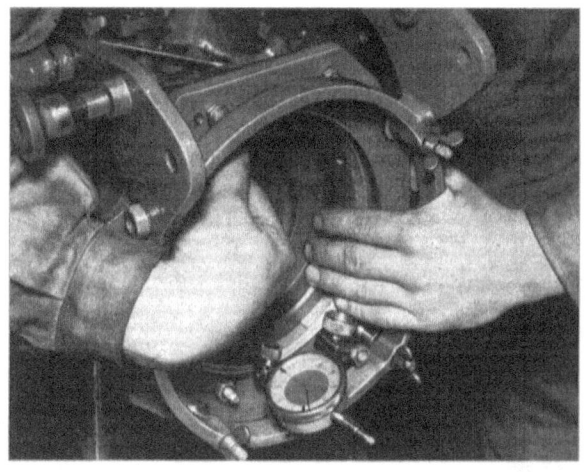

37. Unscrew flywheel nut from flywheel blocked previously by fixture No. 498 (see No. 10 to 23).

Caution: To screw on the nut place turned surface towards the flywheel and check flywheel for tight fit by moving it to and fro. If the tapered shaft end does not fit well give it a short lapping treatment. After installation check flywheel clutch face squareness and out-of-round of crankshaft end with the aid of a dial gauge. Max. out-of-squareness 0.08 – 0.1 mm = .0032" to .004".

Fig. 52

38. Remove flywheel. (flywheel puller No. 311, ring spanner 27 mm)

Fig. 53

Caution: When assembling make certain that the flywheel key does not sit upon flywheel.

39. Remove 5 screws fixing flange of front bearing cover plate. (socket spanner 10 mm)

Fig. 54

40. Heat engine crankcase on a plate or in an over up to about 100 to 120° C = 210 to 250° F.

Fig. 55

41. Place connecting rod so that the big end stands at the recess machined in right-hand border of crankcase aperture and remove crankshaft by turning it slightly upwards.

42. Immediately thereafter expel camshaft bearing by pushing the warm crankcase against a hard wood plate (work-bench).

Isetta Factory Repair Manual

The reassembly is carried out in precisely the reverse order.

For individual treatment of connecting rod, piston, valves, crankshaft and oil pump see under M 12, M 14, M 20, M 24 and M 26

M12 Replacing connecting rod bushing
(Engine is removed, cylinder and piston are dismounted from engine, gudgeon pin bushing is pressed in)

Fig. 56

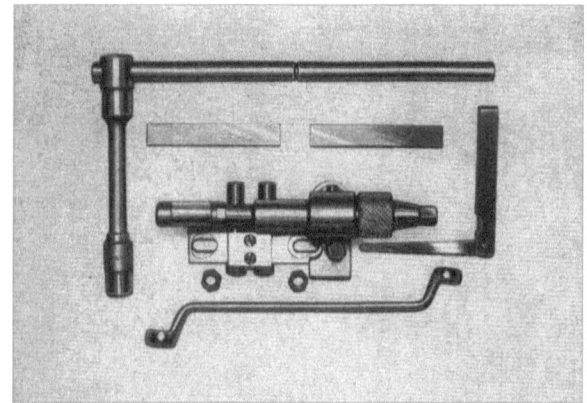

Tools: Hunger reaming tool for rod bushings, socket spanner 14 mm, ring spanner 14 mm, parallels for alignment of connecting rods 5036, drift for gudgeon pin 5002, feeler gauge.

Fig. 57

1. Install Hunger reaming tool and fix it with two nuts 14 mm. (socket spanner 14 mm)

2. Slacken eccentric shaft and align small end with tapered end of reaming tool. (ring spanner 14 mm)

Fig. 58

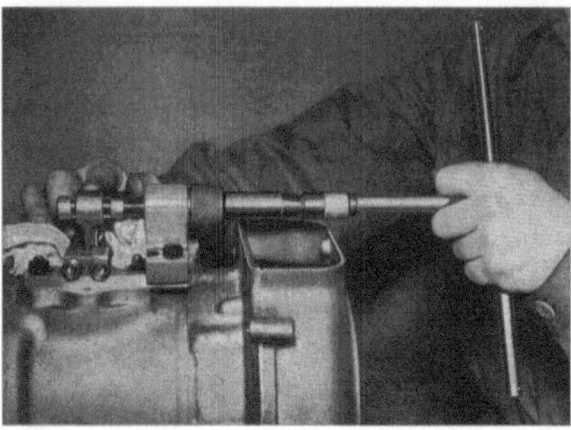

3. Tighten eccentric shaft. (ring spanner 14 mm)

4. Ream rod bushing with reaming tool. (socket spanner 14mm)

Caution: Seal crankcase well with rags.

Fig. 59

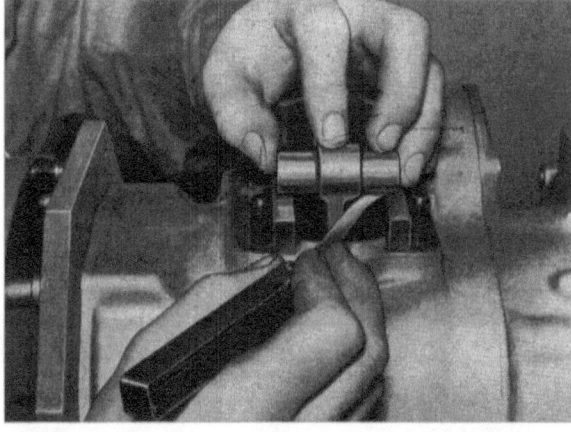

5. Enter gudgeon pin and check position of connecting rod with the aid of two parallels and feeler gauge or by means of a visual test. (2 parallels L 5036, feeler gauge)

Caution: If the connecting rod must be straightened, apply the two rod straightening tools only on the upper third of connecting rod. A correct and careful treatment of the rod bushing obviates any further alignment.

Fig. 60

6. Heat piston on a plate or in oil up to 60° C=140° F, warming gudgeon pins slightly at the same time.

7. Enter piston pin with the aid of drift. (gudgeon pin drift 5002)

Isetta Factory Repair Manual

Caution: Place piston in correct position, arrow on top of piston must regard in direction of the timing case.

Caution: When fitting a new piston and pin assembly use always items bearing the same identification colour marks.

M 14 Installing new cylinder
(old cylinder is removed, new piston fitted)

Fig. 61

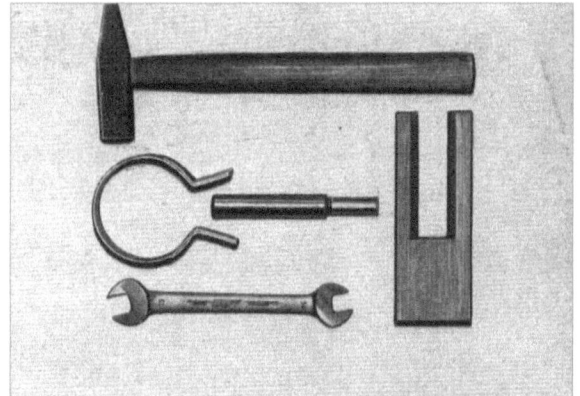

Tools: Piston ring compressor, piston board, drift to adapt pushrod covering tubes No. 530, open ended spanner 14 mm, hammer.

1. Place cylinder base gasket upon crankcase, rough side towards housing.

Fig. 62

2. Protect piston by piston board and compress piston rings by means of the piston ring compressor. (piston board, piston ring compressor)

Caution: Oil piston rings around.

3. Adapt the cylinder and slide it down together with the piston ring compressor.

Fig. 63

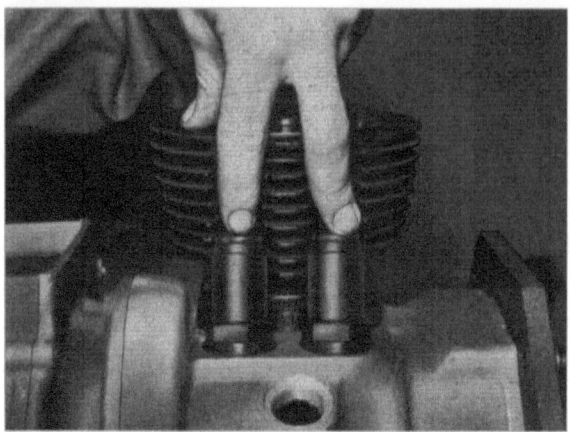

Caution: Make certain that the rubber grommets on the tappet guides engage well and fit evenly upon these units.

Fig. 64

4. Replace cylinder base nuts and tighten them in a diagonal order to secure even tightness. (open ended spanner 14 mm)

Caution: After a short operation period tighten the four base nuts again.

Fig. 65

5. In case a gap is left between rubber grommet and tappet guide tap the pushrod covering the tube slightly down by means of the special drift N. 530.

M 20 Adjusting valves

Fig. 66

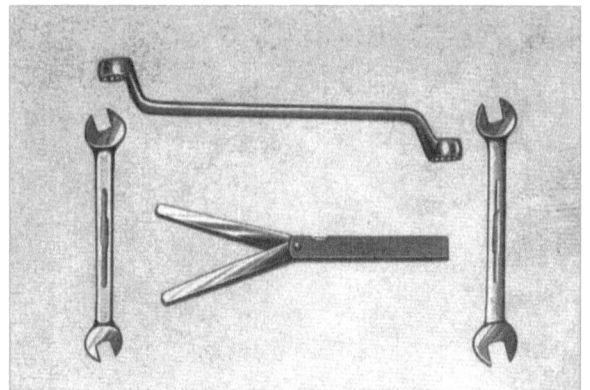

Tools: Ring spanner 14 mm, open ended spanner 2x12 mm, feeler gauge 0.15/0.20 mm, sparking plug spanner.

Fig. 67

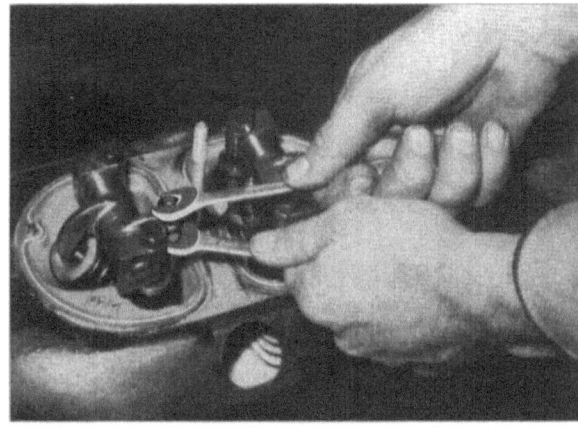

1. Remove screw plate giving access to sparking plug and valves.

2. Withdraw shielded terminal of high-tension lead and unscrew sparking plug. (spark plug spanner)

3. Remove rocker covers. (ring spanner 14 mm)

4. Set engine by rotating the blower wheel to T.D.C. compression, in which position the two valves are closed.

5. Slacken locknut of valve clearance adjusting screw. (2 open ended spanners 12 mm)

Fig. 68

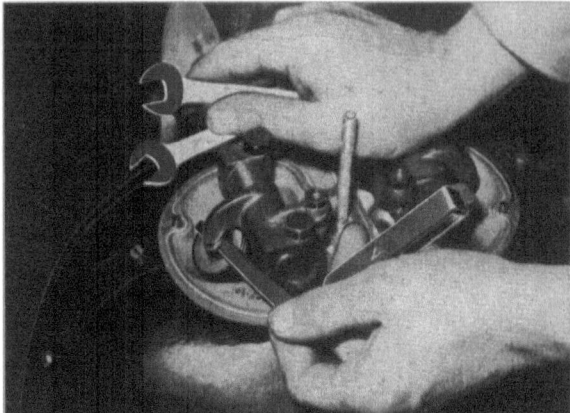

6. Using feeler gauge check valve clearances, 0.15 mm = .006" for intake valve at left (timing case side), and 0.2 mm = .008" for exhaust valve at right (flywheel side). (feeler gauge)

Fig. 69

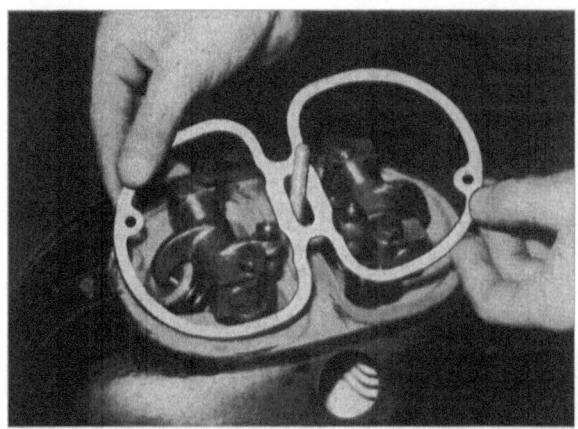

7. To adjust the clearance, if it is found to be incorrect, screw adjuster pin up or down as required until the correct amount of play is felt. The feeler gauge must slide easily between rocker end and valve stem when being drawn fore and aft.

8. Secure obtained position of adjusting pin by tightening the locknut.

9. When locknut is properly tightened, check the play again with the feeler gauge, to make certain that it has not been altered while tightening the nut. Rectify the play if necessary.

10. Check rocker cover gasket, and if it is found to be worn, discard it.

Fig. 70

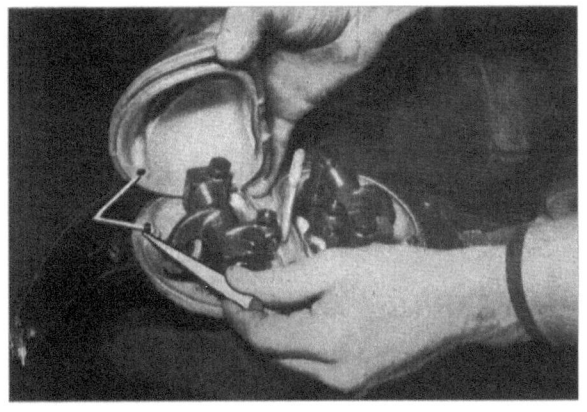

11. Replace rocker covers.

Caution: Be sure to install rocker covers in a way that the cover locating pins on the cylinder head fit correctly in the corresponding drill holes in rocker covers. This is necessary to ensure freedom from distortion and consequent oil leakages. (ring spanner 14 mm)

13. Replace sparking plug and shielded terminal of high-tension lead.

14. Replace inspection aperture cover plate.

M 22 Overhauling cylinder head
(Cylinder head is removed)

Fig. 71

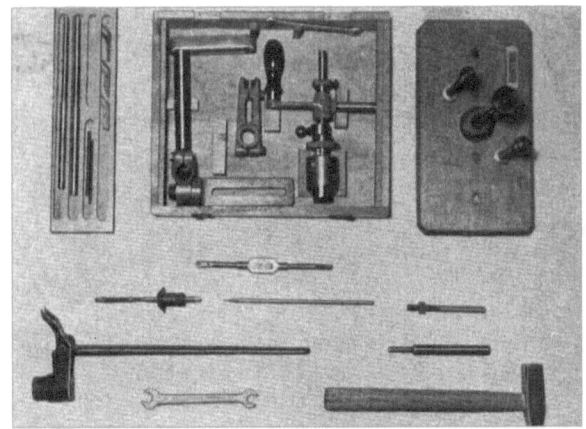

Tools: Holding board for intake and exhaust valves No. 361a, valve spring lifter V 5034, valve reseating tool Hunger, valve grinding equipment, scriber, hammer, drift, heating plate.

Fig. 72

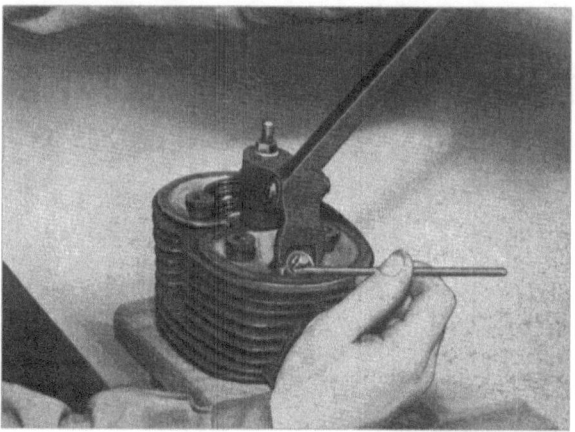

1. Place cylinder head upon wooden block. (holding board No. 361a)

2. Install valve spring lifter. (tool V 5034)

3. Compress the valve springs until the split collets can be removed. (scriber)

Fig. 73

4. Withdraw valve springs, raise cylinder head from the board and remove the valves.

5. Remove valve guides.

<u>Caution</u>: Cut or turn valve guide on spring side down to the retaining circlip, remove circlip and with the aid of a drift expel the old guides towards the combustion chamber. To enter the new guides heat cylinder head assembly up to about 220° C = 425° F. Secure the new valve guides by means of the retaining circlips.

6. Using reaming too ream each valve guide to 7 mm = .28 inch plus a maximum of 0.085 mm = .0034 inch of clearance.

7. Apply Hunger valve reseating equipment and rectify the seats.

Fig. 74

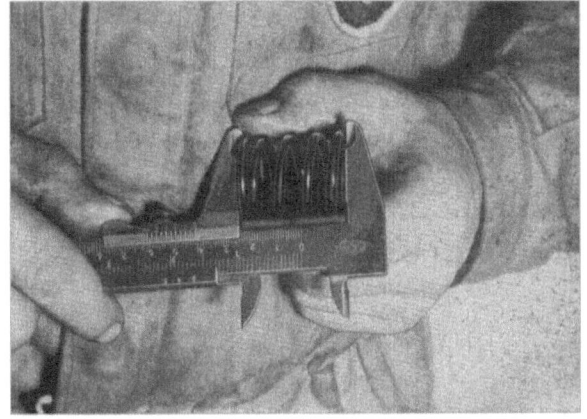

Caution: Valve seat width 1.5 to 2 mm = .06 inch to .08 inch, re-cut seatings with cutting tool 45 deg. Determine the width of seat by using a 15 degree cutter at the top, and a 75 degree cutter at the bottom.

8. Measure unloaded length of valve springs. Length of long spring 42.3 mm = 1.763 inch, length of short spring 37.5 mm = 1.48 inch. Discard springs that do not meet the above requirements.

Fig. 75

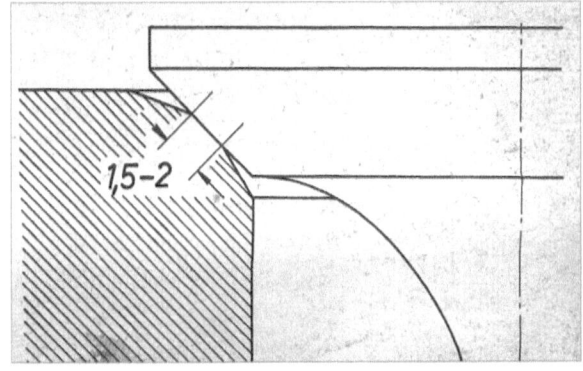

Caution: When reassembling valve springs, make certain the closed coils are toward the cylinder head.

9. Grind valves with the valve refacing equipment.

Caution: The application of the Hunger valve reseating and refacing equipment obviates the treatment with a grinding compound.

10. When the seat is properly positions, it must contact the middle portion of valve face. To recondition the seat with respect to the face of valve apply cutters 15 degree and 75 degree, as shown in Figure 75.

M 24 Overhauling crankshaft
(Crankshaft assembly with bearings is removed)

This job should only be carried out by those servicemen who possess the necessary special tools and the knowledge to apply them correctly. In all other cases, install a replacement crankshaft assembly.

Fig. 76

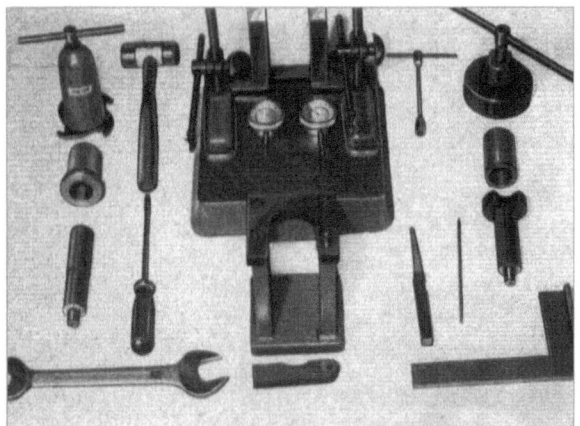

Tools: Socket spanner 10 mm, open ended spanner 32 mm, special tools for crankshaft overhaul 467, 282, 353 A-C, 493/1-4, 531, 524, feeler gauge, screwdriver 8 mm, square, scriber.

Fig. 77

1. Remove flange with oil pipe from front bearing cover plate, four screws. (socket spanner 10 mm)

2. Install puller No. 467 and remove front bearing cover. (socket spanner 10 mm, Matra puller 467)

Fig. 78

3. Unscrew slotted head screw from oil thrower disc. (screwdriver 8 mm)

Caution: When refitting oil thrower disc secure slotted head screw by a punch blow. The oil thrower disc must attach evenly on the counterweight face.

4. Remove oil thrower disc with slight blows of a plastic hammer.

5. Remove ball bearing from flywheel bearing cone. (puller No. 282, open ended spanner 32 mm)

Fig. 79

6. Install bushing compensating thickness of shaft. (bushing No. 531)

7. Place crankshaft upon test equipment and check tapered shaft ends for true rotation. Out-of-true limit on shaft ends is 0.02 mm = .0008 inch. (crankshaft testing equipment No. 353 A, two indicator dials with stand 353 B and 353 C).

Fig. 80

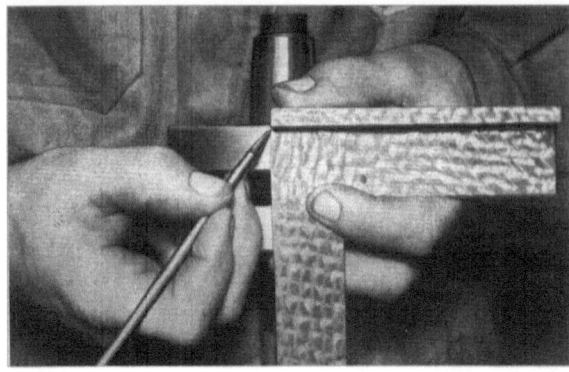

Caution: If the crankshaft is found to run out of true it can be recentralized. This job, however, should only be carried out by those servicemen who learned it at the BMW Service Department's training school.

8. Mark crankshaft cheeks to ensure their correct location when assembling. (square, scriber)

Fig. 81

9. Separate the two crankshaft halves by removing crankpin with the aid of a press. (press tool No. 493, intermediary piece No. 493/3, drift No. 493/1)

10. Check crank pin for trueness. Maximum allowable out-of-round 0.003 mm = .00012 inch.

Fig. 82

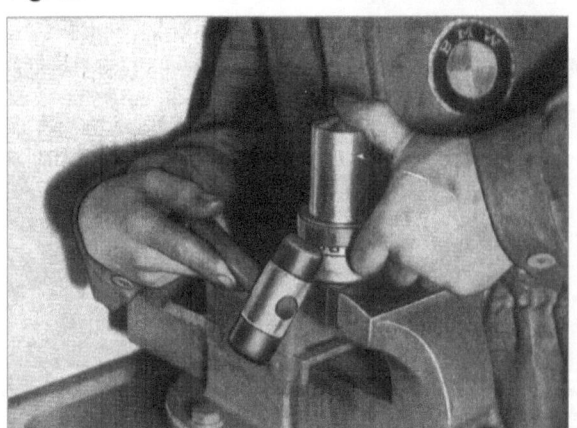

11. Remove connecting rod from crankpin. (holding bushing No. 493/2, plastic mallet)

Isetta Factory Repair Manual

Fig 83

Caution: To replace con rod upon crankpin use replacer No. 524.

For the sizes of connecting rods and big-end roller bearings see spare parts list.

Fig. 84

12. Lap connecting rod if necessary. (lapping arbour V 5046)

Fig. 85

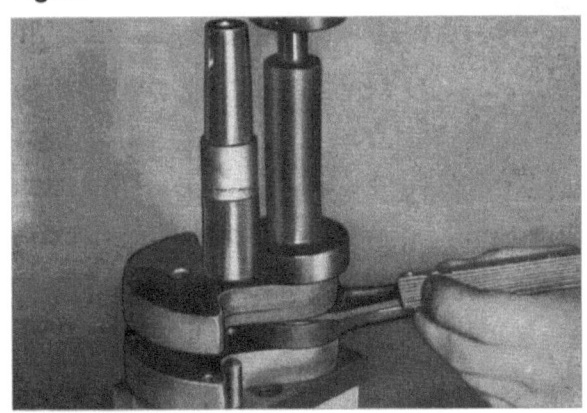

13. Assemble crankshaft with hydraulic press.

Caution: Apply press tool No. 493/1 in reversed condition. Insert feeler gauge 0.05 mm = .002 inch between big end and counterweight. Compress until the feeler gauge just can be removed.

61

Insert intermediary piece below counterweight to prevent distortion of crank pin.

14. Heat ball bearing to about 60°C = 140°F and slide it upon crankshaft end journal.

M 26 Overhauling oil pump

Fig. 86

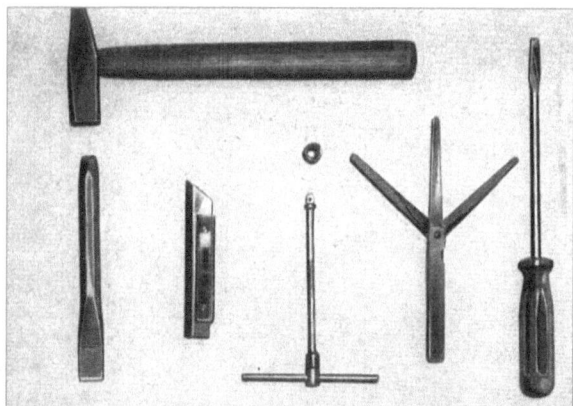

Tools: Hammer, socket spanner 10 mm, screwdriver 10 mm, feeler gauge 0.03/0.04 and 0.05 mm = .0012/.0016" and .002", straightedge.

Fig. 87

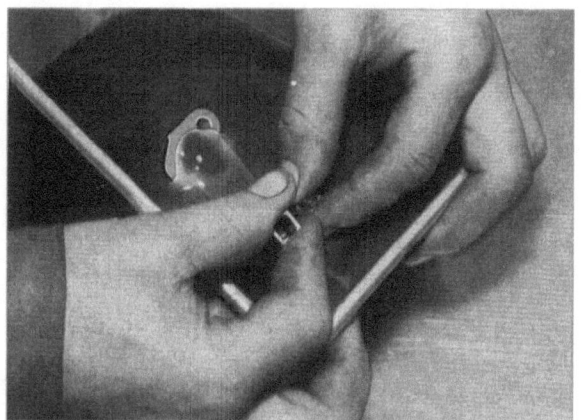

1. To check oil pump dip in oil so that the gears are beneath the oil level and rotate it clockwise by means of the drive. When turning with the fingers oil must ooze out of the oil outlet orifice.

Fig. 88

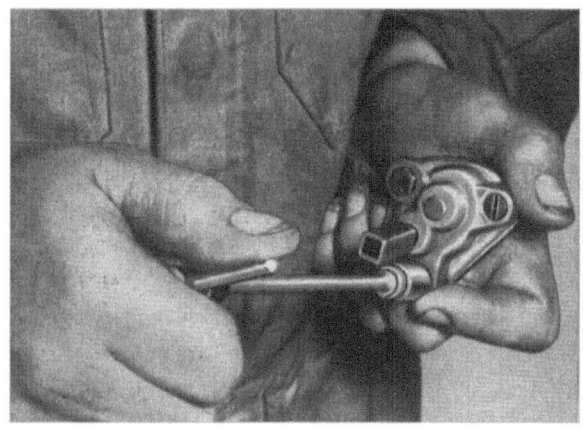

2. Straigten bent ears of oil screen lock washer. (hammer, chisel)

Caution: During all these jobs hold pump with the hand, do not put it in a vice.

3. Remove oil screen (socket spanner 10 mm)

Caution: When assembling place oil strainer assembly at the attachment flange, the strainer opening outwards, insert the connection washer.

4. Straigten bent ears of pump screws locking washers. (hammer, chisel)

5. Remove pump fixing screws. (two screws, socket spanner 10 mm, one screw, screwdriver)

Fig. 89

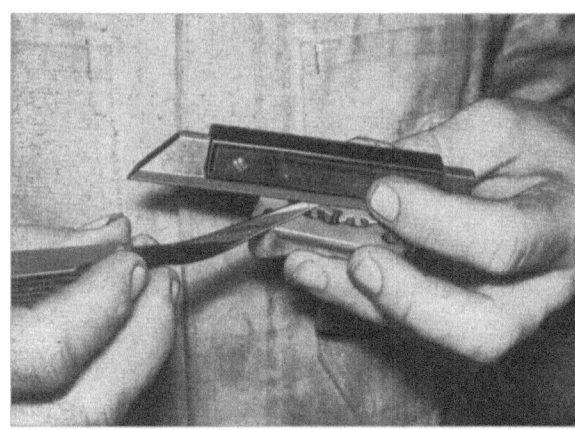

Caution: After assembling secure slotted head screw by a punch blow.

6. Measure clearance over pump gears. Maximum allowance clearance 0.03 to 0.04 mm = .0012 to .0016 inch. (straightedge, feeler gauge)

Fig. 90

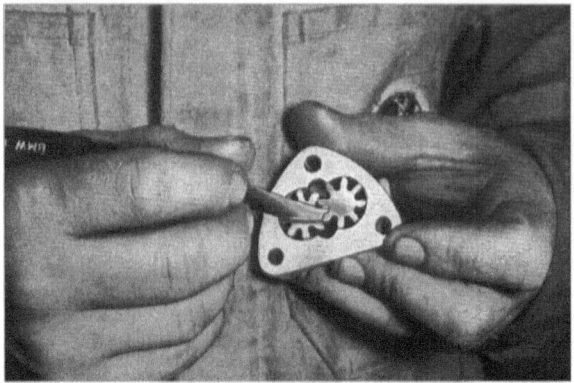

7. Check clearance between gears (backlash) 0.03 to 0.05 mm = .0012 to .002 inch. (feeler gauge)

Caution: If the bottom plate is scored owing to rotation of pump gears, the bottom surface may be rectified until clearance below straightedge will disappear.

M 30 Adjusting ignition timing

Fig. 91

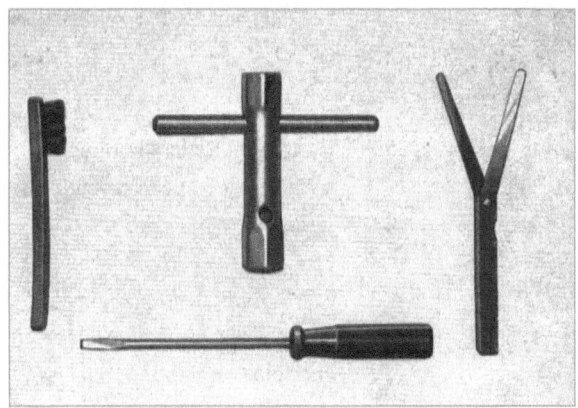

Tools: Sparking plug spanner, sparking plug steel brush, screwdriver 6 mm, feeler gauge 0.4 to 0.6 mm = .016 to .024 inch.

Fig. 92

When resetting ignition timing also clean sparking plug and readjust electrode gap.

1. Remove screw plate giving access to sparking plug.

2. Withdraw spark plug connector and unscrew sparking plug.

3. Clean sparking plug and adjust electrode gap to 0.6 mm = .024".

4. Remove cover from blower wheel. (screwdriver 6 mm)

5. Rotate blower wheel in a clockwise direction until the colour marked blade registers with the mark "S" on the housing of the blower unit.

6. Continue turning the blower wheel until the breaker contact points are fully opened.

7. Check contact breaker gap with the contact gauge (0.4 mm = .016").

Fig. 93

8. If the gap is too big or too small, slacken the stationary point locking screw (Fig. 93,1) and turn the eccentric adjusting screw (Fig. 93, 2) until the correct gap is obtained. Then tighten lock screw.

Fig. 94/95

9. Slacken the two contact breaker plate securing screws and turn the blower wheel until the colour-marked blade meets the mark "S" on the blower housing.

10. Disconnect back-coloured contact breaker lead from terminal 1 of ignition coil and connect the test lamp with one pole to terminal 1 of ignition coil and the other to the connector end of the disconnected black lead.

11. Push in ignition key to switch on ignition and move the contact breaker plate in direction of rotation until the lamp lights up. Then move contact breaker plate carefully contrary to rotation direction until the lamp just goes out.

12. Tighten the contact breaker plate in this position by means of the two locking screws (Figures 94/95).

13. Remove test lamp, reconnect the contact breaker lead to terminal 1 of ignition coil and replace the blower wheel cover. (screwdriver)

14. Replace sparking plug, push cable connector upon sparking plug and reposition screw plate upon the inspection aperture.

GROUP G
TRANSMISSION

G3 Dismantling and assembling transmission
(Transmission is removed)

Fig. 1

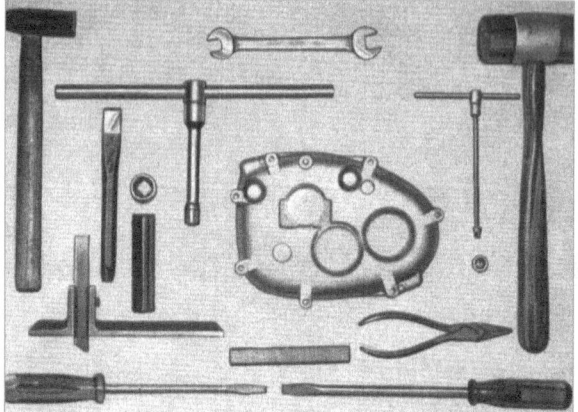

Tools: Hammer, chisel, two big screwdrivers, open ended spanner 14 mm, socket spanners 10 and 19 mm, plastic mallet, wooden tool, cotter pin pliers, depth gauge, guiding plate for installation of transmission shafts toolkit illustration No. 30.

Fig. 2

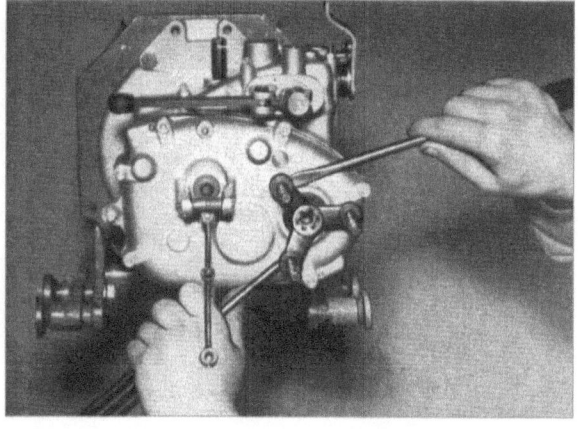

1. Locate transmission on support fixture and drain oil. (socket spanner 19 mm)

2. Withdraw clutch rod from hollow center of drive shaft towards the clutch end.

3. Release tab washer for the coupling flange fixing screw. (hammer, chisel)

4. Unscrew coupling flange fixing screw. (socket spanner 19 mm)

5. Remove coupling flange with the aid of 2 screwdrivers.

Isetta Factory Repair Manual

Fig. 3

6. Unscrew the nuts securing transmission rear and cover. (socket spanner 10 mm)

7. Remove rear cover by means of a wooden drift.

Caution: Apply wooden tool only on the provided drift lobes right and left, never attempt to remove the cover by inserting a screwdriver blade or similar tool between the castings.

Fig. 4

Caution: When refitting the cover make certain that the pin holding reverse idler shaft enters the slot machined in bearing housing. Likewise be sure that the thrust bearing on clutch rod end applies correctly in its seating. Insert clutch rod to centralise the bearing.

Fig. 5

8. Drive ball bearing out of the cover plate by gently heating the plate and dropping it – joint face downwards – on a wooden block.

Caution: Before replacing the cover on reassembly fit heated ball bearings upon the shafts and enter the bearing and shaft assemblies into their bearing housings by means of soft blows with a plastic mallet. (plastic mallet)

9. Measure bearing height with respect to the bearing cover by means of a depth gauge and on assembling compensate the difference by placing spacing shims behind the bearings.

Fig. 6

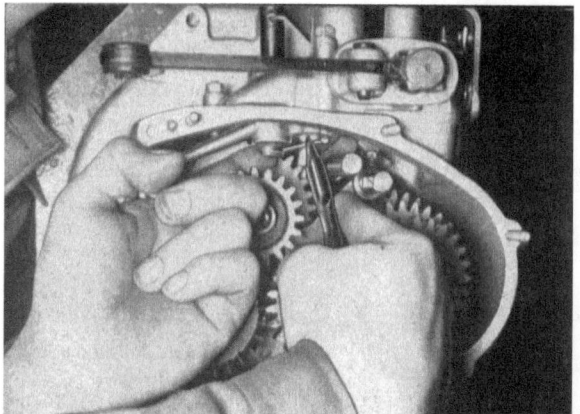

10. Remove cotter pin from the pivot of the lever that operates the reverse selector shaft.

11. Unscrew nuts of transmission top cover bearing the gearshift selector mechanism. (socket spanner 10 mm)

Fig. 7

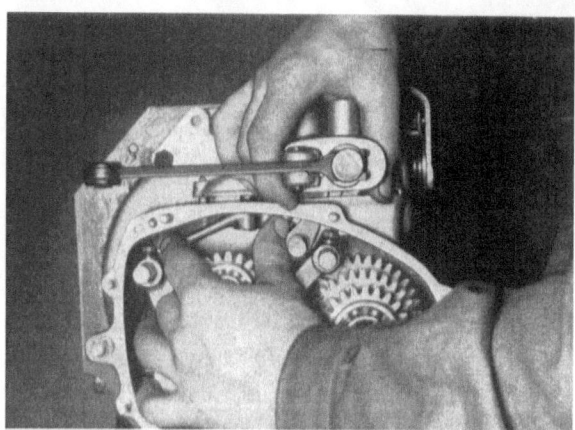

12. When removing top cover draw reverse fulcrum level situated at the inner side of top cover downwards.

Caution: When replacing transmission top cover refit the fulcrum level simultaneously from beneath.

Fig. 8

Caution: Before refitting the cover place the selector forks in neutral position and fulcrum level in central position.

Fig. 9

13. Remove gearshift selector ball springs and the detent balls.

Fig. 10

14. Remove the two lock screws which hold selector forks to selector shafts. (socket spanner 10mm)

Fig. 11

15. Withdraw selector shafts and lift out selector forks.

16. Unscrew slotted plug for spring and detent ball of reverse selector shaft. (screwdriver 8 mm)

Fig. 12

<u>Caution</u>: When assembling secure slotted plug by means of a center punch blow.

17. Remove spring and detent ball for reverse selector shaft.

18. Slide out reverse idler shaft with idler gear and selector shaft.

Fig. 13

19. Remove all other shafts by heating transmission case to about $60°$ C = $140°$ F upon a heating plate.

<u>Caution</u>: To replace the shafts on reassembly use template toolkit illustrated No. 30 so the shaft and ball bearing assemblies will enter with proper alignment.

20. Remove ball bearings and dismantle the shafts.

Fig. 14

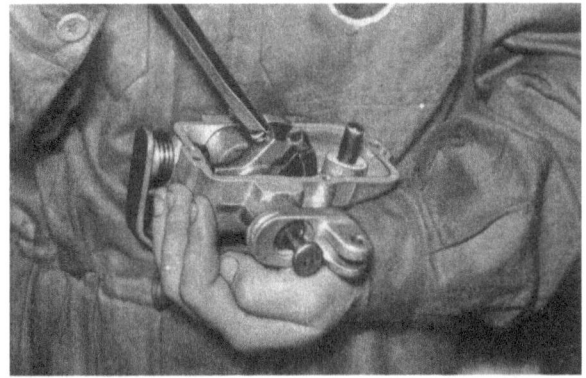

21. Dismantle selector (top) cover:

    a) Unscrew slotted plug for detent spring. (screwdriver 8 mm)

    b) Remove detent spring and ball.

    c) Remove cotter pin from selector level. (cotter pin pliers)

    d) Remove selector level.

    e) Unscrew slotted head screw serving as pivot for the fulcrum lever of guide shaft sector and withdraw the fulcrum lever.

Fig. 15

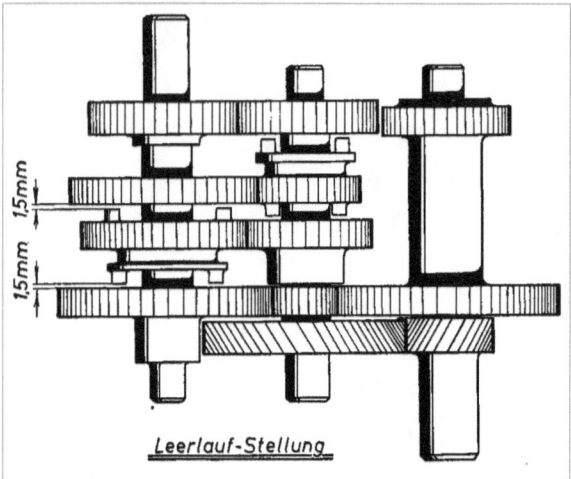

f) Remove fulcrum lever holding sector and the selector guide shaft.

> Caution: Take care not to lose the two spacing shims at the right and left of the connecting sector on selector guide shaft.

g) Remove gear change operating lever by slackening the nut on inner side of housing, remove spring. (open ended spanner 14 mm)

The reassembly is carried out in precisely the reverse order.

The two dog clutch units set in neutral position must have a clearance of 1.5 mm = .06 inch on either side.

G5 Adjusting gear control linkage

Fig. 16

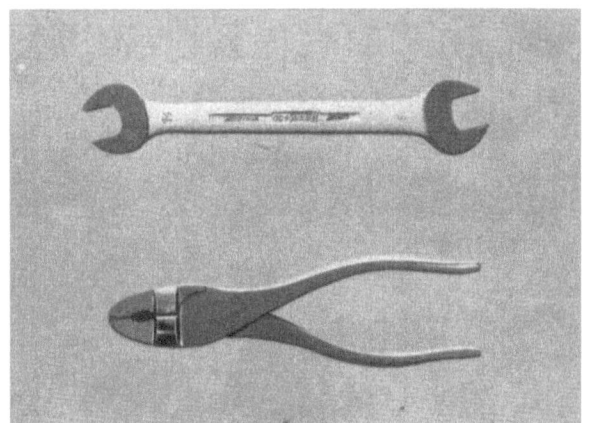

Tools: open ended spanner 14 mm, pliers.

Fig. 17

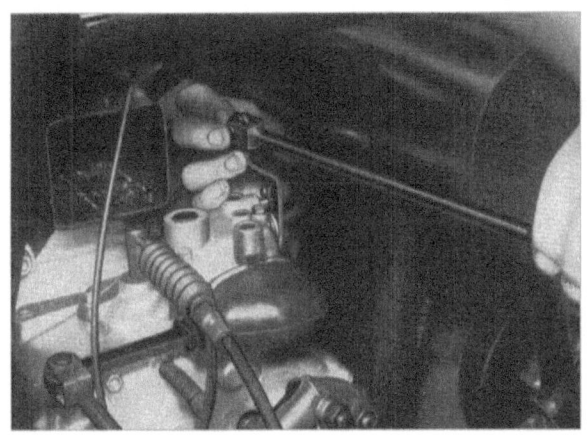

1. Place gear lever at the left of the seat in neutral position, the operating lever on the transmission must be placed against the engine.

Fig. 18

2. Approach gear lever rod to the connecting lever, so that the toggle pin enters smoothly. If this position is not obtained slacken lock nut and rotate toggle (clevis) until the toggle pin fits correctly.

Fig. 19

3. Now adjust the two transverse rods in precisely the same manner by slackening the lock nut and turning the toggle (clevis) unit until the desired position is obtained.

Fig. 20

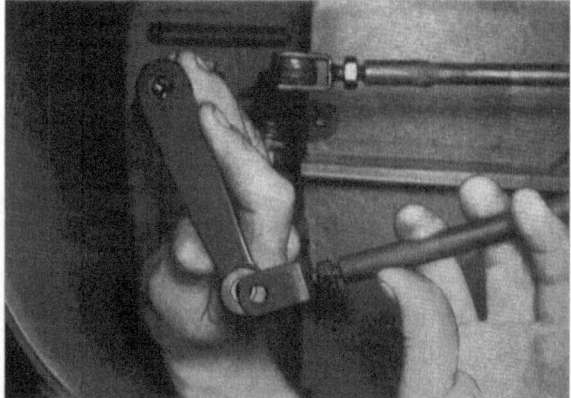

GROUP H
REAR AXLE

H1 Removing and refitting rear axle

Fig. 1

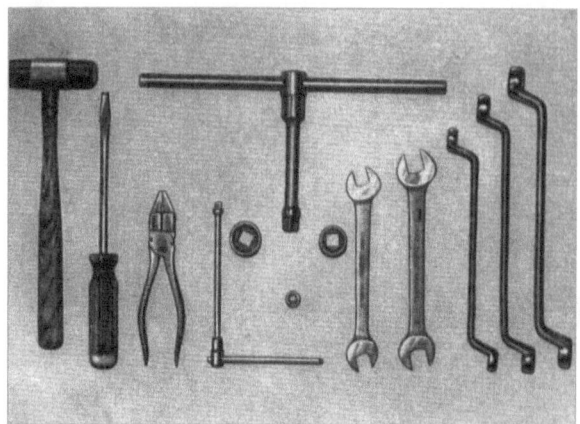

Tools: Wheel nut spanner, open ended spanners 12/14/17 mm, socket spanners 9/14/19/22, ring spanners 12/17 mm, screwdriver 6/8 mm, cotter pin pliers, circlip pliers, hammer, chisel, plastic mallet.

Fig. 2

1. Drain oil from rear axle case. (ring spanner 12 mm)

2. Remove seat and rubber mat.

3. Remove handbrake lever support unit. (four screws, socket spanner 9 mm)

4. Remove cotter pin from handbrake lever pin and withdraw the lever pin. (cotter pin pliers)

Fig. 3

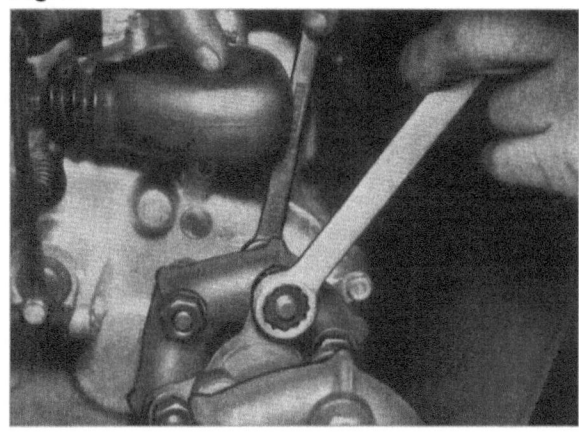

5. Push handbrake cable back through body panel.

6. Remove cover plates from the rear wheels, slacken wheel nuts. (screwdriver, wheel nut spanner)

7. Support the vehicle at rear by applying the jack under the engine carrying cross members.

8. Unscrew the nuts from three bolts on rubber coupling at transmission end. (ring spanner 17 mm and open ended spanner 14 mm)

Caution: These three bolts must be slackened which connect the rubber ring to the three-legged coupling flange on gearbox shaft.

Fig. 4

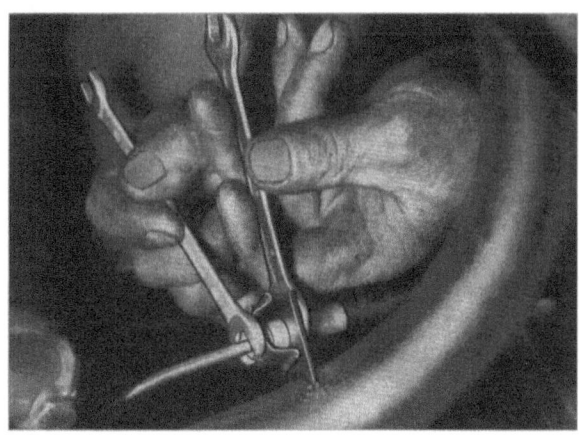

9. Detach brake cable hose from holding bracket. (open ended spanner 17 and 12 mm)

Fig. 5

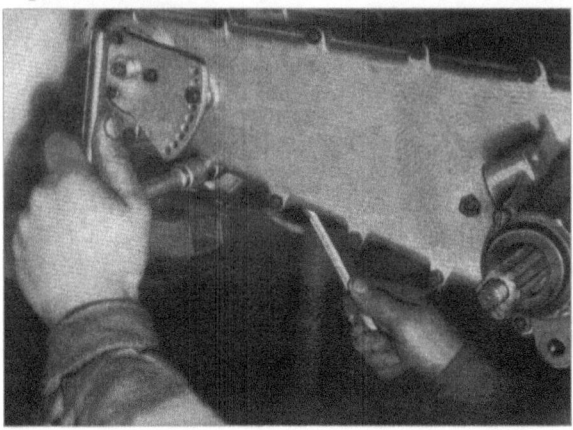

10. Remove clip fixing handbrake cable hose on right-hand rear leaf spring. (screwdriver)

11. Remove cotter pins and unscrew the nuts securing telescopic shock absorbers on rear axle casing, at right and lift. (cotter pin pliers, ring spanner 17mm)

12. Remove cotter pin from thorough bolt crossing chaincase and swing link connecting the assembly to the chassis frame. Unscrew nut of thorough bolt. (cotter pin pliers, ring spanner 14 mm, open ended spanner 14 mm)

13. Unscrew speedometer drive on front end of chaincase.

14. Unscrew spring-eye bolt of left-hand cantilever spring. (socket spanner 19 mm)

Caution: When assembling tighten this bolt carefully until it gets stopped as otherwise the thread in the aluminum case would be torn out.

15. Unscrew nut of right-hand spring eye bolt. Press the bolt out.

16. Remove rear axle unit rearwards by turning it in a clockwise direction.
The reassembly is carried out in precisely the reverse order.

Caution: After refitting bleed and adjust the hydraulic brake system.

H2 Dismantling and assembling rear axle assembly
(Rear axle assembly removed)

Fig. 6

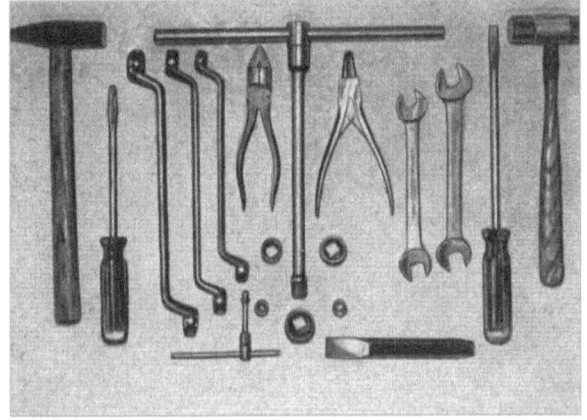

Tools: Open ended spanner 14 mm, socket spanners 9/10/14/22 mm, ring spanners 10/19 mm, screwdriver 8/12 mm, cotter pin pliers, circlip pliers, hammer, chisel, plastic mallet.

Fig. 7

1. Remove cotter pins from rear axle nuts, right and left. (cotter pin pliers)

2. Unscrew axle nuts, right and left. (socket spanner 22 mm)

3. Remove the two hubs. (screwdriver and plastic mallet)

4. Remove screw securing wheel cylinder and brake adjuster on brake plate. (ring spanner 10mm)

5. Remove brake shoe assemblies, unhook handbrake cable.

6. Remove the brake plate from rear axle case. (screwdriver 11 mm)

Fig. 8

7. Remove adjuster plate for chain tensioner. (socket spanner 9/10 mm)

8. Remove chain case bolts, 6 thorough bolts 14 mm with nuts, nine screws 10 mm. (socket spanner and open ended spanner 14 mm, socket spanner 10 mm)

Fig. 9

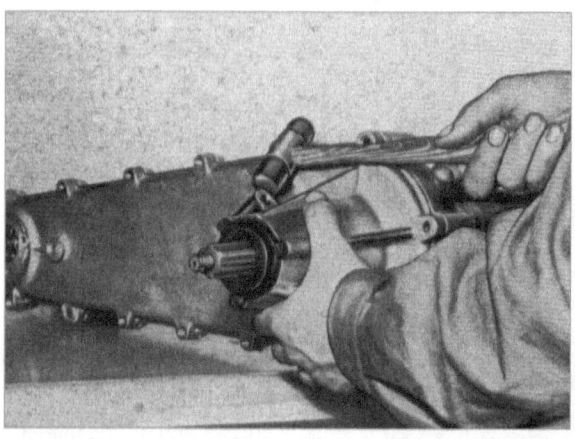

9. Loosen case half by gentle blows of a plastic mallet against the joint line and remove the part with the shorter axle housing extension.

Caution: When disassembling and assembling the chain case castings never tap against the housing border, but apply soft blows with a plastic mallet against the shock absorber anchor noses as shown of figure. When assembling pay attention to the fit of eccentric for chain adjustment. Heat chain case gently on the ball bearing seat.

Fig. 10

10. Remove the two bearing shells from rear axle.

Caution: When assembling make certain that the flange end of split bearing collar regards inwards.

Fig. 11

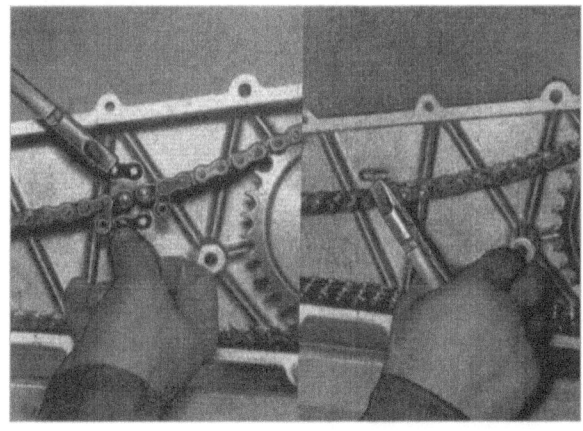

11. Loosen chain lock and remove chain by turning the shafts.

Caution: When assembling the chain make sure to refit the chain lock in correct position. The hardened (blue) member of the connecting link must be fitted in the middle and the browned one at front. The spring fastener must always be put on with the closed end facing the forward direction of travel of the chain.

Fig. 12

12. Remove long back axle case extension from right-hand chain drive casting by means of a plastic mallet.

Caution: To remove this axle casing tap also against the shock absorber nose, on no account jam a screwdriver blade between the castings as this would damage the joint faces.

Fig. 13

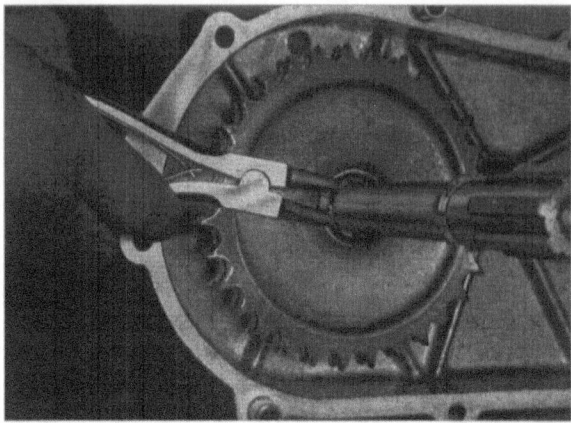

13. Remove circlip securing rear sprocket. (circlip pliers)

Fig. 14

14. Remove rear axle sprocket frontwards by means of screwdrivers and plastic mallet.

15. Remove circlip behind the sprocket. (circlip pliers)

16. Remove rear axle in contrary direction by tapping it with a plastic mallet.

<u>Caution</u>: When carrying out these jobs the casting must be well supported on the spots where the parts in question are located.

17. Release lock tab of tab washer for screw fixing three-legged coupling flange to front sprocket drive shaft. (hammer and chisel)

18. Remove the above screw at the rubber joint. (ring spanner 19 mm)

19. Withdraw three-legged coupling flange from front sprocket drive shaft. (two screwdrivers)

20. Remove chain tensioner.

21. Detach carrier for rubber sealing washer on chain tensioner. (screwdriver 8 mm)

22. Press out front sprocket shaft.

Fig. 15

23. Remove ball bearings from all castings integrating the rear axle assembly.

Caution: Remember that all aluminum castings must be heating before removing and refitting the ball bearings. Use a heating plate to heat them up to about 60 to 70° C = 140 to 160° F. Do not attempt to drive or to press out a ball bearing.

The reassembly is carried out in precisely the reverse order.

H4 Adjusting Chain

Tool: Open ended spanner 10 mm

Fig. 16

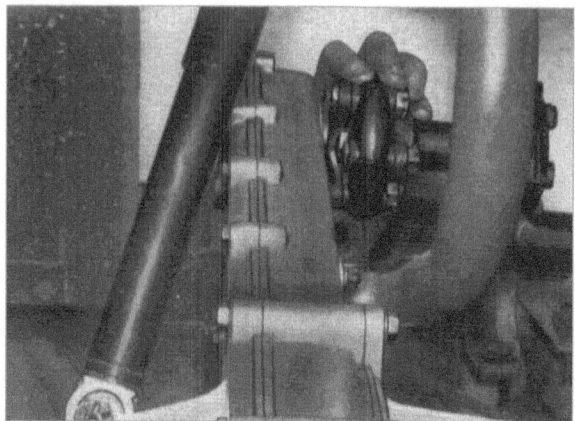

Caution: To check the chain for stretch proceed as follows: Place gears in neutral position, grasp the rubber coupling with the hand from beneath and turn it with short movements in clock and anticlockwise directions. If the slack is being increased, one notes this condition by the chain's striking against the chaincase during the alternative movement.

Fig. 17

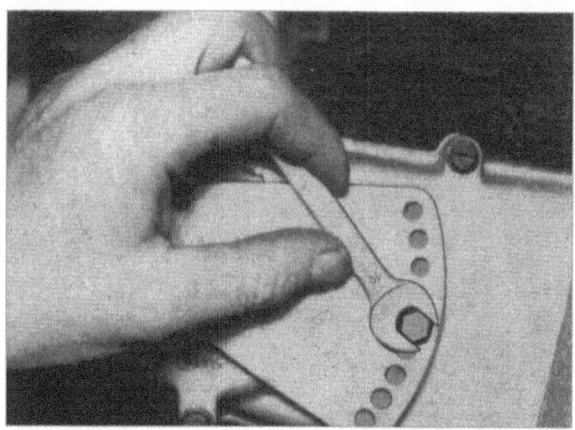

The readjustment is then carried out in accordance to the instructions below:

1. Remove adjuster plate locating screw. (open ended spanner 10 mm)

Isetta Factory Repair Manual

Fig. 18 & 19

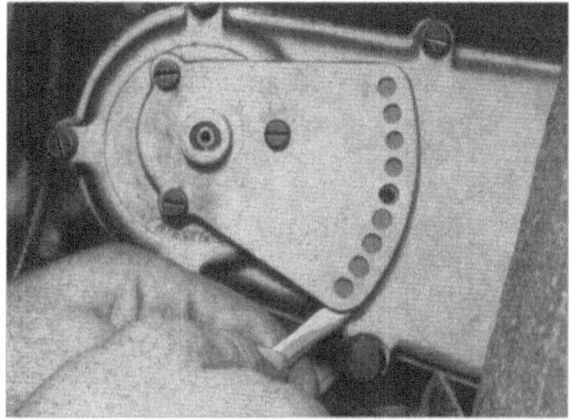

2. Raise the adjuster plate with a screwdriver until the holes register

Caution: The holes must precisely coincide so the locating screw can be provisorily screwed in with the hand. Never try to force in the locating screw as thus one would risk to smash the thread in the aluminum casing. If the correct coincidence of the holes cannot be obtained, return the adjuster plate to the next suitable hole.

Fig. 20

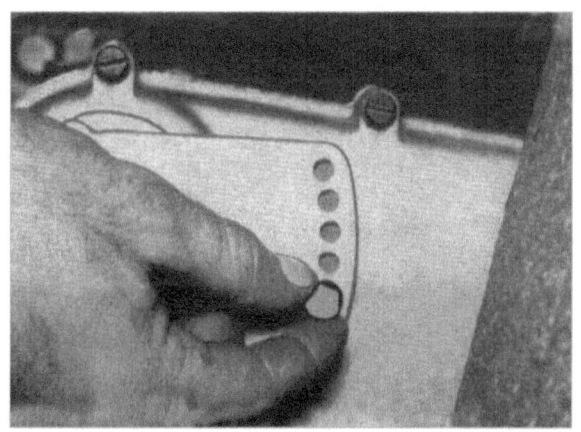

3. Screw the locating screw in with the hand and tighten it with a spanner. (open ended spanner 10 mm)

4. Check double-roller chain again for correct tension by moving it as indicated above.

H6 Replacement of chain

Fig. 21

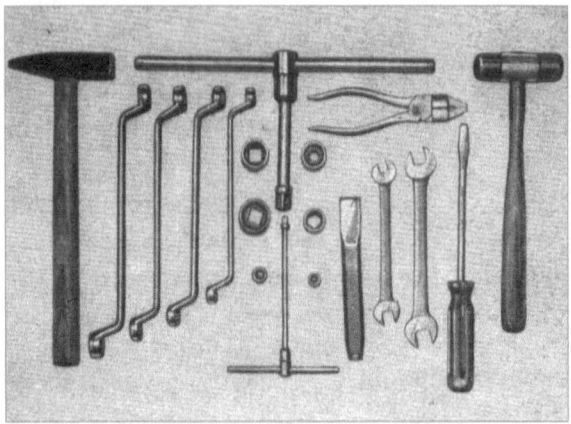

Tools: Wheel nut spanner, open ended spanner 10/14 mm, socket spanners 9/10/14/17/19/22 mm, ring spanners 10/12/14/17 mm, screwdriver 6 mm, cotter pin pliers, hammer, chisel, plastic mallet.

Fig. 22

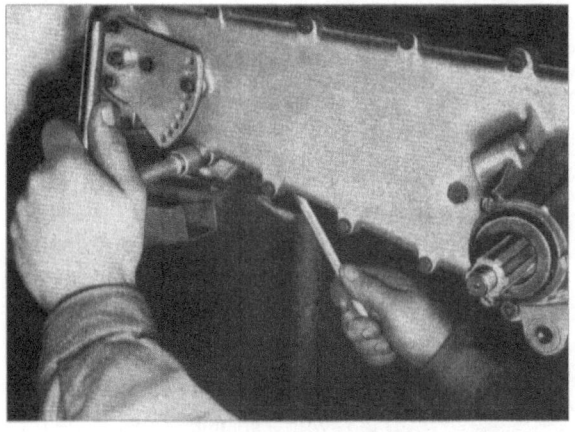

1. Drain oil from rear axle case. (ring spanner 12 mm)

2. Remove cover plate from left-hand rear wheel, slacken wheel nuts. (screw driver, wheel nut spanner)

3. Raise the vehicle at rear by placing a suitable support under the frame member beneath the engine.

4. Remove left-hand rear wheel.

5. Detach left-hand mudguard, 2 screws top, 2 screws on bottom. (ring spanner and open ended spanner 10 mm)

6. Remove left-hand rear spring (see F3).

7. Remove left-hand shock absorber (see F4).

8. Loosen speedometer connection.

9. Remove cotter pin and unscrew the rear axle nut. (cotter pin pliers, socket spanner 22 mm)

10. Press-off the wheel hub and drive it out. (screwdrivers and plastic mallet)

11. Detach chain tensioner adjusting plate. (socket spanner 9 and 10 mm)

12. Support right-hand rear axle casing additionally by a suitable arrangement.

13. Remove cotter pin and unscrew thorough bolt crossing chaincase and swing link. (ring spanner and open ended spanner 14 mm)

Fig. 23

14. Remove the screws connecting the two chaincase halves. (socket spanners 10 and 14 mm, ring spanner 14 mm)

15. Loosen left-hand casting by gently tapping the joint line with a plastic mallet and drive the casting outwards. (plastic mallet)

Caution: Do not attempt to remove the casting by inserting a screwdriver blade or a chisel between the castings as such as procedure would damage the joint faces. When removing and replacing the cover do not tap against the border of casting, but only against the noses for spring and shock absorber attachment. On reassembly make certain that the chain tensioner eccentric is fitted in correct position.

Fig. 24

16. Slacken the chain completely.

17. Remove chain lock spring fastener and open the chain lock.

<u>Caution</u>: When assembling the chain make sure to refit the chain lock in correct position. The hardened (blue) member of the connecting link must be fitted in the middle and the browned one at front. The spring fastener must always be put on with the closed end facing the forward direction of travel of the chain.

Fig. 25

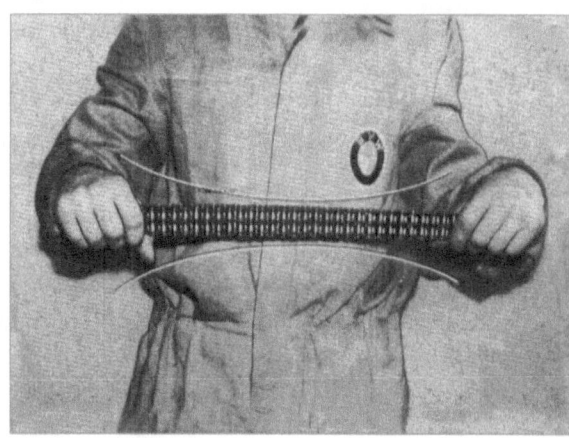

18. Remove the chain by rotating the wheel.

<u>Caution</u>: The chain is checked for wear by bending it laterally. If the lateral bending curves are found to be too high as shown on figure 25, the chain must be discarded.

The reassembly is carried out in precisely the reverse order.

GROUP V
FRONT SUSPENSION

V1 Removing and refitting a front suspension assembly

Fig. 1

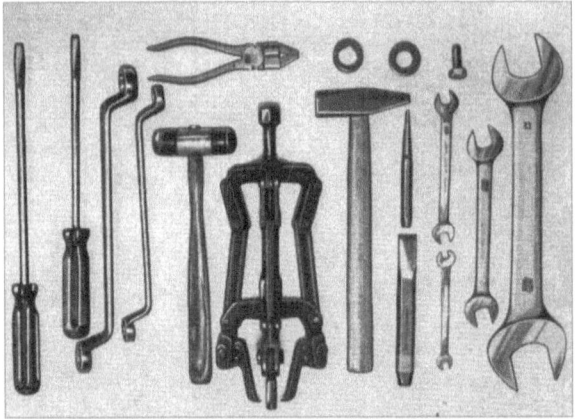

Tools: Open ended spanners 7/10/11/17/36 mm, screwdriver 10 mm, ring spanners 17/19/22 mm, pliers, hammer, chisel, drift 6 mm, plastic hammer, screw 10x1 mm, tube pieces, washers, commercial-type puller.

Fig. 2

1. Remove wheel cover plate, slacken wheel nuts, jack-up the vehicle.

2. Remove wheel and brake drum.

3. Remove dust cap. (open ended spanner 36 mm, large screwdriver or tire lever)

Fig. 3

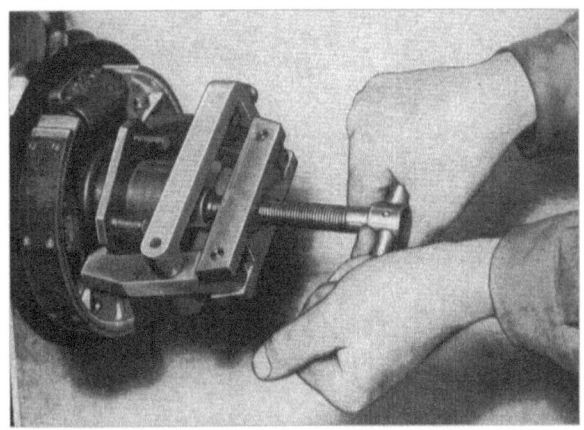

4. Remove cotter pin from hub nut. (cotter pin pliers)

5. Unscrew hub nut. (ring spanner 22 mm)

6. Remove wheel hub with the aid of a commercial-type puller.

Fig. 4

7. Remove the spacer washer on steering knuckle (tub axle).

8. Detach brake hose on wheel cylinder. (open ended spanner 17mm)

Fig. 5

9. Slacken two screws fixing wheel cylinder assembly, on inner side of brake support. (open ended spanner 10 mm)

10. Slacken the two screws securing the adjusting cam assemblies, at inside bottom of brake support. (open ended spanner 10 mm)

11. Remove rubber cap from bleeder screw.

12. Remove brake shoes with wheel cylinder and adjusting cam assemblies.

Caution: To remove the brake shoes enter the two forefingers in the center holes, so that the linings will not be soiled by grease or oil.

Fig. 6

13. Remove screws fixing dust cover for oil seal. (open ended spanner 7 mm)

14. Remove dust cover and oil seal assembly.

Caution: When assembling make certain that the recess serving as outlet for the oozing oil is fitted downwards.

Fig. 7

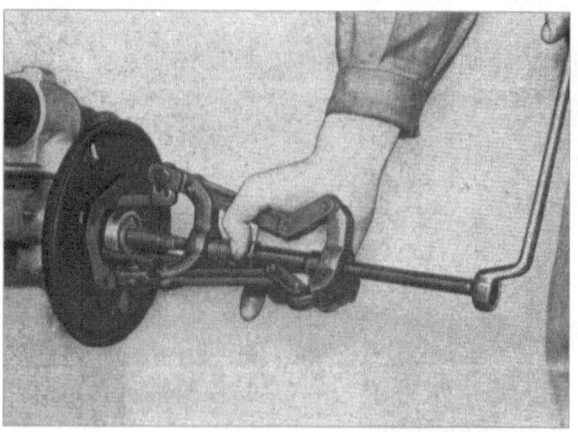

15. Remove ball bearing from steering knuckle (commercial-type puller)

Fig. 8

Caution: When assembling replace ball bearing with the aid of a suitable tube piece applied against the inner race of ball bearing.

16. Remove the four slotted-head screws fixing brake support. (screwdriver 10 mm)

17. Remove the big slotted-head screw for reception of break reaction on support plate. (large screwdriver)

18. Unscrew the nut from spring rod shaft. (open ended spanner 17 mm)

19. Drive out spring rod shaft by means of a plastic mallet or with a brass drift, if very tight.

Fig. 9

20. Release lock tab of tab washer for swing arm fulcrum shaft. (hammer and chisel)

21. Remove screw from swing arm shaft. (ring spanner 22 mm)

Caution: When assembling make certain that the spacer between swing arm shaft and lock plate is fitted correctly. The lock tab of tab washer must be bent down into the recess on the lock plate border.

Fig. 10

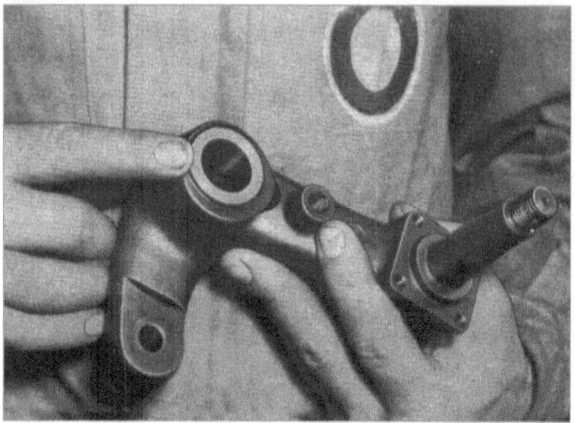

22. Remove swing arm assembly.

Caution: When pressing a new bearing bush into the swing arm unit make sure that the flange side of bushing points outwards, so that the lubrication hole in swing arm coincides with the annular groove in the bushing.

Fig. 11

23. Remove rubber cap for coil spring.

24. Remove cotter pin from the spring rod nut. (cotter pin pliers)

25. Unscrew nut from front end of coil spring rod, simultaneously securing the coil spring rod against distortion. (ring spanner)

Caution: See also Group F Springs and Shock absorbers F1 to 2 and 5.

26. Withdraw spring plate and coil spring.

27. Remove coil spring rod rearwards, remove the spring support bushing with the two rubber buffers by pushing them forward.

Fig 12

28. Remove cotter pin from nut securing track rod bolt. (cotter pin pliers)

29. Unscrew the nut from track (tie) rod bolt. (ring spanner 17 mm, open ended spanner 17 mm to hold the bolt)

29a. On the left-hand front suspension additionally remove cotter pin from nut securing steering drag link bolt, unscrew this nut and remove steering drag link. (ring spanner 17 mm, open ended spanner 17 mm to hold the bolt)

30. Unscrew nut from threaded end of taper key on steering knuckle king pin. (open ended spanner 10 mm)

31. Unscrew grease nipple from steering knuckle king pin. (open ended spanner 11 mm)

32. Drive out the taper key, using a hammer and finally a drift. (hammer, drift)

33. Remove king downwards pin by means of pull screw M 10 x 1, suitable tube pieces and washers. (screw M 10 x1, open ended spanner 17 mm)

Fig. 13

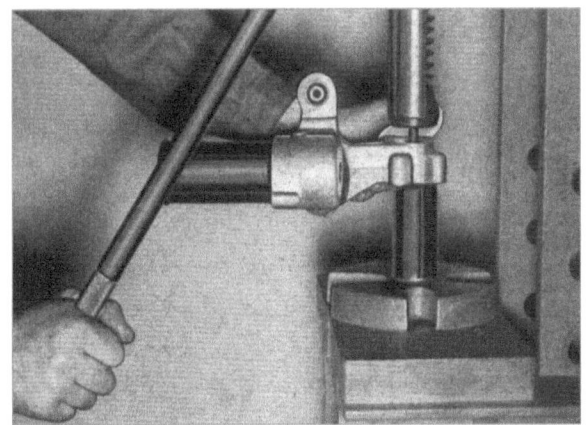

34. Remove steering knuckle.

35. Straighten lock tab of tab washer securing the swing arm shaft. (hammer and chisel)

36. Unscrew nut from swing arm shaft. (ring spanner 19 mm)

37. Remove swing arm shaft with the aid of a press.

Fig. 14

38. Remove wheel hub ball bearing with the aid of a press.

Fig. 15

39. Press out, respectively drive out the king pin bearing bushing.

<u>Caution</u>: To press out this bushing fill the inner space behind the bushing flange with consistent grease to render it airtight and with the aid of the king pin and short blows of a plastic hammer drive the bushing upwards, which will come out through the hydraulic action of the grease stored behind the bushing flange.

V 10/11 Front Wheel alignment, checking toe-in

Fig. 16

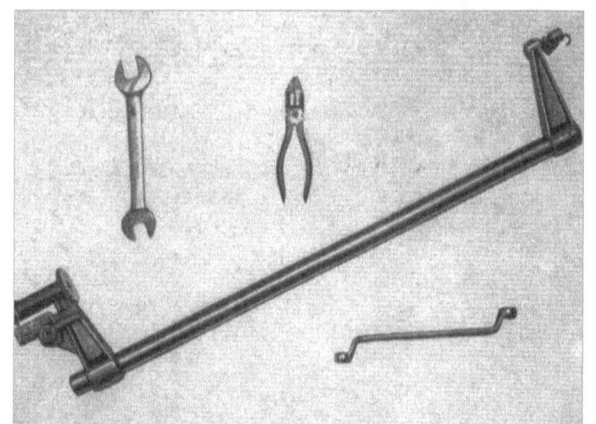

Tools: Toe gauge, ring spanner 17 mm, cotter pin pliers, open-ended spanner 22 mm

Fig. 17

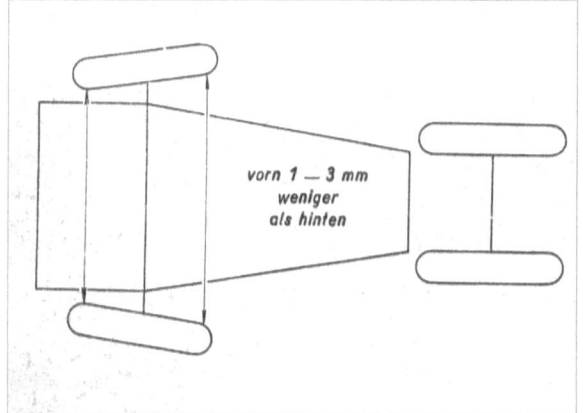

Fig. 18

1. Jam toe gauge between the two front wheel tires.

Fig. 19

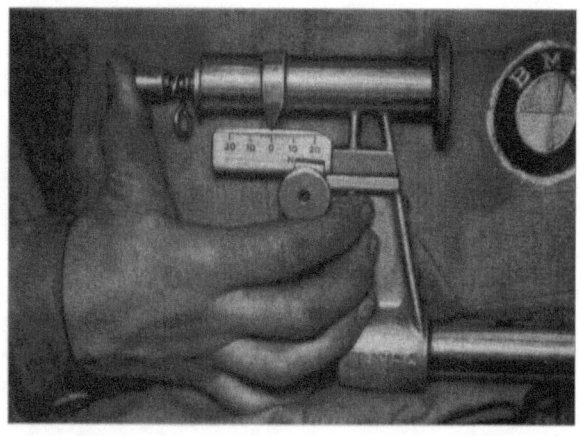

2. Set the indicating pointer to the zero mark on the quadrant.

Caution: In order to provide a clear illustration the adjustment of the indicator arrangement is shown with the track (tie) rod removed.

3. Pull the vehicle ahead until the toe gauge hangs at the same height at rear.

4. Read the difference on the toe gauge quadrant.

Caution: Toe-in, that is the amount the front wheels are closer together at the front than they are at the rear, should be 3 to 5 mm. If the toe-in reading is incorrect, check front suspension for damages. Replace all parts, which are damaged, worn or distorted. Thereupon measure toe again and adjust, if necessary.

5. Slacken lock nut for clevis on left-hand end of track (tie) rod. (open ended spanner 22 mm)

6. Remove cotter pin from nut on left-hand end of track (tie) rod and unscrew this nut. (cotter pin pliers, ring spanner 17 mm)

Fig. 20

7. Adjust the track (tie) rod clevis in order to lengthen or shorten the rod. Rotation by 180 deg. (1/2 turn – 1 mm of toe alteration). Clockwise rotation increases, anticlockwise rotation reduces toe-in.

8. Attach track (tie) rod, tighten clevis bolt nut and repin, and secure with the lock nut.

9. Check toe again.

Isetta Factory Repair Manual

ANNEX FOR EXPORT MODEL 1957

GROUP V
FRONT SUSPENSION
CONTINUED

V1 Removing and refitting one front suspension assembly (with instructions for repair)

Fig. 21

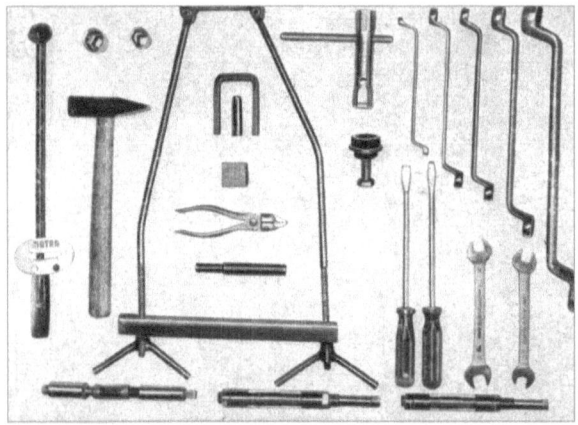

Tools: Ring spanners 7/14/17/19/22/36 mm, box spanner 21 mm with tommy bar, open ended spanners 14/17 mm, 2 screwdrivers, hammer, pliers, hub puller 5090, spring compressor 5091, shock absorber replacer and bow, soft drift, hard wood block 33 mm high, torque spanner with 19 mm and 22 mm sockets, special "Hunger" reamers P 19.8 – 21 ∅ F7, 22 ∅ H 7, 25 ∅ H 7.

1. Remove hub cap, slacken wheel nuts (21 mm) by means of box spanner and raise the vehicle.

Fig. 22

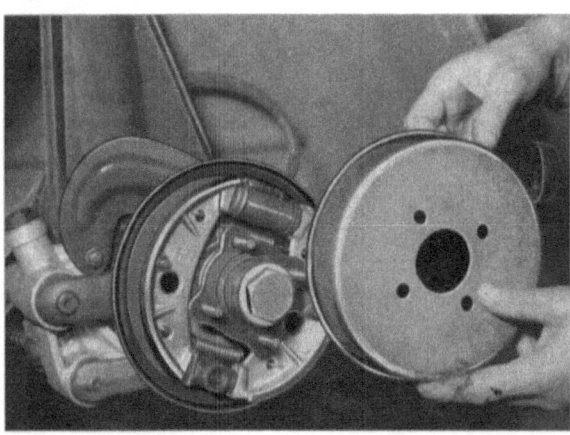

2. Remove wheel nuts and spring washers, withdraw wheel and brake drum.

3. Remove the sealing screw (36 mm), countering with a screw driver on the wheel studs of the hub for this purpose. (See Fig. 2).

Isetta Factory Repair Manual

Fig. 23

4. Remove the cotter pin from the end of wheel spindle and unscrew castle nut with washer (pliers, box spanner 22 mm).

5. Use tool V 5090 to pull hub and bearings off the wheel spindle. Remove washer in front of brake plate.

Caution: When assembling hub, be sure that the dust cap with the grease retaining is centered on the hub. If necessary, loosen screws, which secure the dust cap on steering knuckle, center the dust cap, retighten screws and secure them with a center impact. When replacing the outer ball bearing in the hub, insert a spacer equalizing in thickness the old one, between ball bearing outer race and hub in order to evenly distribute the lateral thrusts to the two ball bearings and to avoid the jamming of the two ball bearings as well. Side clearance .02 - .05 mm = .0008 - .0020".

Fig. 24 & 25

6. Detach brake hose from wheel cylinder. (Only necessary if brake hose, brake plate or wheel cylinder have to be replaced. In this case it will be necessary to bleed the brake system after assembly.)

Fig. 25 & 26

7. Pry off shoes with a screw driver. Do not let oil or grease touch the drum or linings.

Caution: When assembling, make certain that the big holes in the brake shoes are below the spindle center.

Fig. 27

8. Prevent pistons from leaving wheel cylinders by means of a rubber band (a).

9. Remove dust cap and grease retaining from brake plate only if inner ball bearing is left on wheel spindle and grease retainer or ball bearing have to be checked.

Isetta Factory Repair Manual

Caution: When assembling, install the dust cap in a way that the recess serving as outlet points downwards (Fig. 6), center the grease retainer on the hub and secure the screws after tightening with a center impact. Do not mistake the right-hand dust cap for the left-hand one and vice versa, as otherwise the outlet bores will be covered.

10. Remove ball bearing from wheel spindle by means of commercial-type puller. (See Fig. 7)

Fig. 28

11. Disconnect track (tie) rod from steering knuckle. For this purpose remove cotter pin from bolt, unscrew castle nut (17 mm) and remove it together with two washers below and one washer above and the bolt.

Caution: When assembling, tighten castle nut with the wheels in the straight-ahead position.

Fig. 29

12. Disconnect steering drag link from steering knuckle arm.

Caution: When assembling, tighten castle nut with the wheels in the straight-ahead position.

Fig. 30

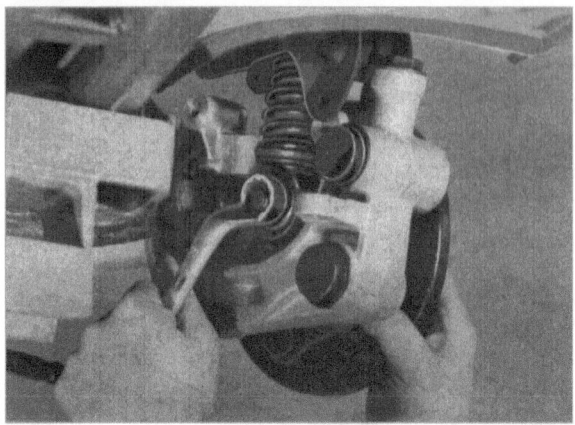

13. Unscrew nut (22 mm) from shock absorber mounting pin on swing arm and remove it together with the washer.

Fig. 31

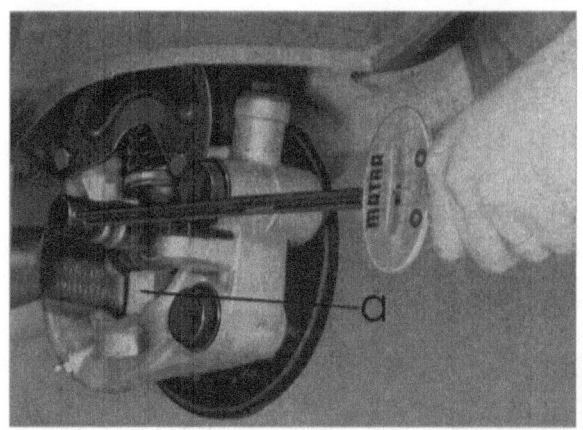

Caution: When assembling, put a 1.3" high wooden block (a) between shock absorber eye and steering knuckle in order to fix the rubber bushing in shock absorber eye in the middle of spring travel, and torque the nut to 58 foot-pounds.

Fig. 32

14. Install spring compressor V 5091 over spring housing and steering knuckle, compress by means of the wing nuts as far as to allow the two fixing bolts to be removed without tension from the steering knuckle after removal of nuts (14 mm). Release the two wing nuts simultaneously and remove the spring compressor.

Fig. 33

Caution: When carrying out repairs, replace the still existing spring housing retaining bolts M 8 x 60 8 K by those with a resistance grade of 10 K and torque to 22 foot-pounds.

Fig. 34

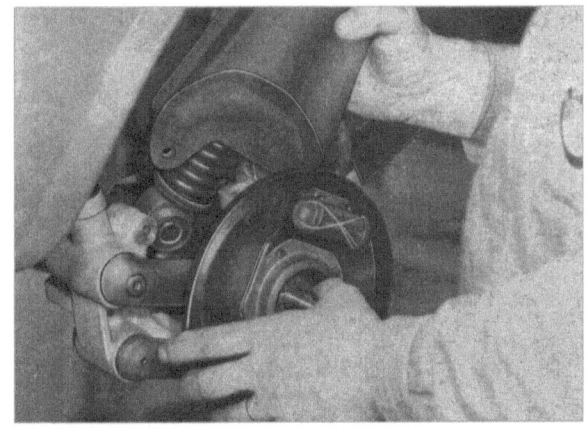

15. Remove spring housing and shock absorber assembly from pin on swing arm.

16. Disconnect brake plate stay from brake plate after removal of nut and spring ring (replace lock washers, if fitted, by spring rings).

Fig. 35

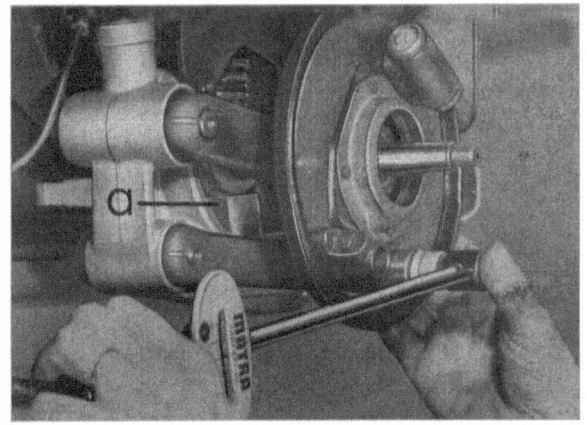

Caution: When re-assembling, put a 1.3" high wooden block (a) between shock absorber eye and steering knuckle in order to fix the rubber bushing in shock absorber eye in the middle of spring travel, and torque the nut to 58 foot-pounds.

Fig. 36

17. Unscrew nut (14 mm) from taper key on steering knuckle pin and take it off with circlip washer. Turn steering knuckle fully inwards and drive out taper key with a soft drift.

<u>Caution</u>: When assembling, fit taper key, so that after tightening the nut the taper key does not protrude, neither on steering knuckle at front nor on nut at rear.

Fig. 37

18. Pry out steering knuckle pin by means of two screwdrivers applied as shown on Figure 37.

(To remove king pins with small grip heads use puller V 5105 – to be made corresponding to drawing supplied).

If it is impossible to pull out the king pin, even with the aid of a commercial puller, drive it out upwards by using hammer and drift. In this case it will be necessary to replace the upper busing in steering knuckle by an upper closed end bushing with bottom collar, because the dust cap installed before will not seal a second time. Equalize the seat of the tapped out dust cap in the steering knuckle. After having pressed in this replacement bushing, ream its bore to 20.02 – 20.04 mm (F7), using reamer P 19.8 – 21 mm ⌀

Fig. 38

19. Pull brake carrier plate from wheel spindle and remove rubber seal ring.

Caution: When assembling, insert rubber seal ring in groove of brake carrier plate, so as to avoid jamming of seal ring.

Fig. 39

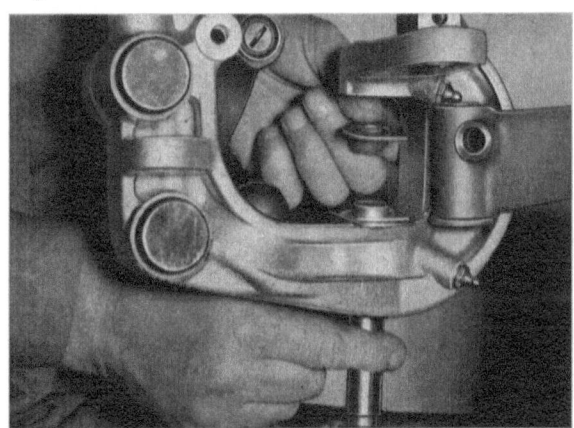

20. Lift steering knuckle out of frame eye, remove spacer and lower distance washer.

Fig. 40

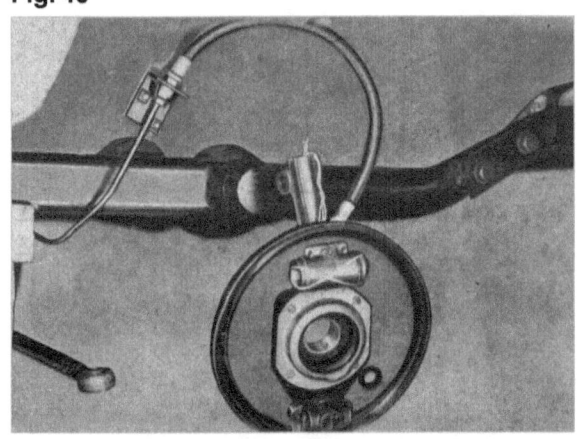

Caution: When re-assembling, choose an upper distance washer as required for a clearance of .05 mm (.002"). If a bottom-collar type upper bushing has been fitted, the clearance of .05 mm can be obtained by inserting shims of suitable thickness beneath the lower distance washer.

Suspend brake carrier plat on frame eye by fastening it with a wire.

Fig. 41

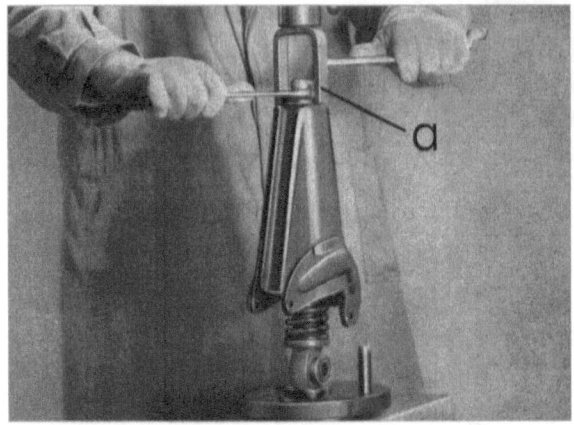

21. Using arbour press and U-piece (a) 5092 between press tool and spring housing, compress shock absorber and spring housing assembly so far that the two holding-down nuts (17 mm) of shock absorber can be removed. Remove rubber grommet with cap and release the spring from pressure.

Fig. 42

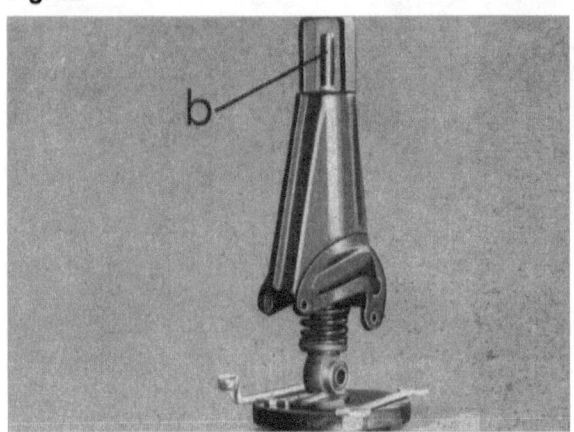

Caution: To install spring housing on shock absorber screw on replacer arbour (b) 5093.

Fig. 43

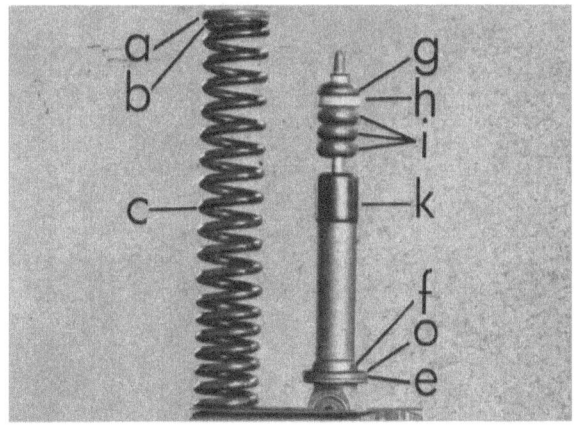

22. Remove spring housing, upper rubber washer (a), guide washer (b), spring (c) and lower washer (o), rubber washer (e), and spring plate (f) from shock absorber.

Caution: When assembling, install multirate coil spring with closer spacings downwards. On the vehicles of future series the rubber washers (a) and (e) as well as the washer (o) will be superseded. This requires a new type of shock absorber with firmly fitted dust shield (k) and lower spring plate.

23. Check shock absorber in vertical position for a steady drag in both directions. The higher tensile force on rebound movement as well as the lower pressure force on compression stroke should prove to be constant over the whole lift. If there are jerking motions there exists a defect requiring replacement. In case of replacement remove rubber grommet (g), stop plate (h), three rubber cushions (i) and dust shield (k) from shock absorber.

Caution! In fully compressed position no pressure over 1 pound should be exercised on the shock absorber, as otherwise interior defects might be caused.

24. If the bushing in shock absorber eye requires replacement, press in the new one so that it flushes with the shock absorber eye on one side.

Fig. 44

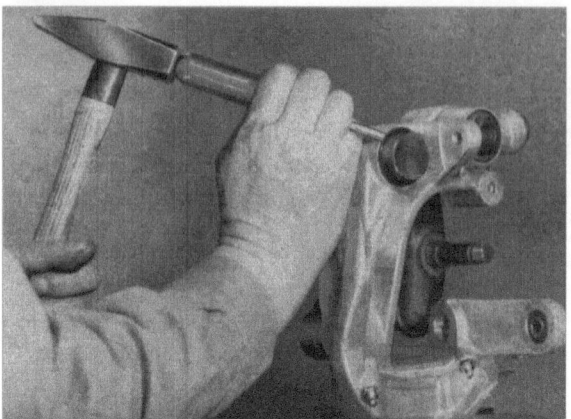

25. Remove swing arm from steering knuckle. Pry off the dust cap by means of a screwdriver.

Fig. 45

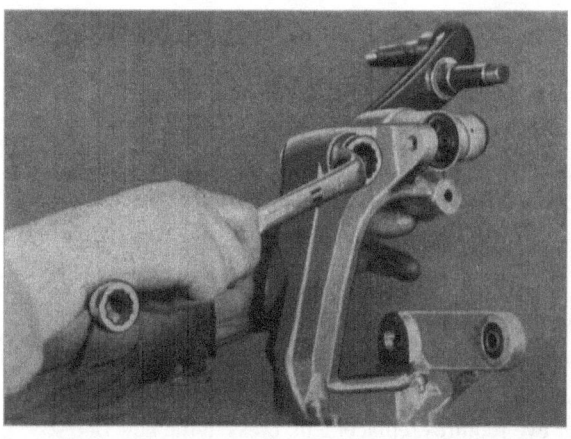

Caution: When assembling, fit dust cap with a non-hardening type of sealing compound.

Unlock tab washer on nut, unscrew nut (22 mm), remove tab washer and lock plate. Remove swing arm from steering knuckle. Remove rubber seal ring.

Caution: When assembling, insert rubber seal ring in groove of steering knuckle, so as to avoid jamming of seal ring.

Fig. 46

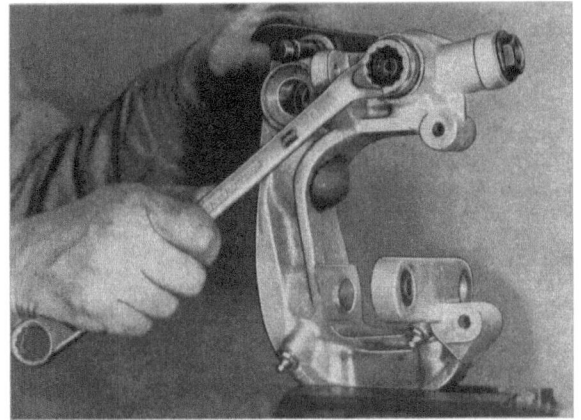

26. Remove brake carrier plate from steering knuckle. Same operations as described under paragraph 25, dealing with swing arm removal.

Fig. 47 & 48

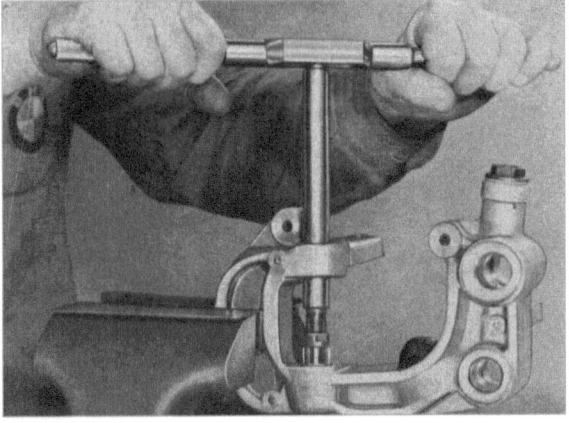

27. To replace bushings in steering knuckle:

a) remove bushings for steering knuckle king pin by driving them inwards with a suitable drift. Drive out dust cap from below upwards and equalize upper portion of bore in steering knuckle. Press new bushings in from inside. Ream upper bushings with bottom and collar by means of reamer P 19.8 – 21 mm ⌀ to 20.02 – 20.04 mm ⌀ (F7). Press also lower bushing from inside in steering knuckle, so far as to allow 1.8 mm to protrude. Ream lower bushing to 20.02 – 20.04 mm ⌀, using upper bore as guide for the reamer (reamer K 19.8 – 21 mm ⌀).

Fig. 49

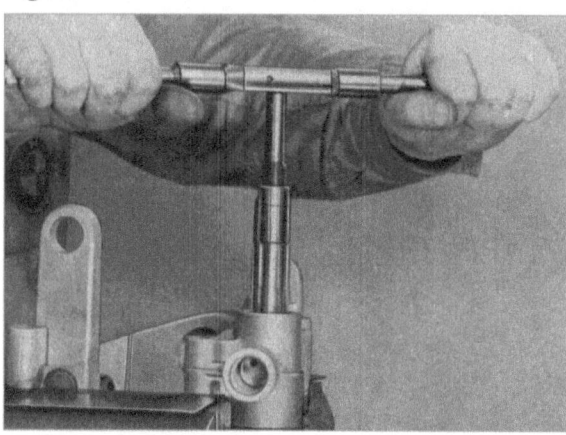

b) Remove bushings for swing arm and brake plate stay by tapping them outwards.

Press in new bushings so that they flush outside, and ream them subsequently, guiding the reamer alternately in left-hand and right-hand bushing bore for this operation.

Bushing bore diameters, new: Swing arm bushing 25.00 – 25.02 mm ∅ (H7), reamer D 24-27.5 mm.

Brake plate stay 22.00 – 22.02 mm ∅ (H7), reamer D 21 – 24 mm.

Fig. 50

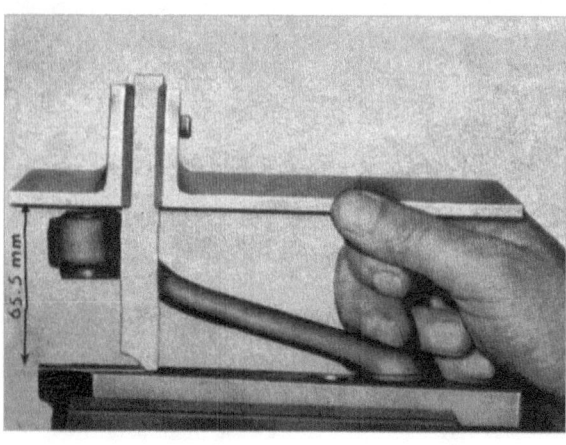

28. If the rubber bushing in brake plate stay requires replacement, press in the new one so far that the distance between bearing face on steering knuckle and contact face of brake plate carrier equals 65.5 mm ± .2 mm. (Measuring gauge 5113 to be made corresponding to drawing supplied).

29. Front wheel alignment and toe-in adjustment as described for Standard model (Fig. 16-20).

GROUP L
STEERING

L1 Removing and refitting steering

Fig. 1

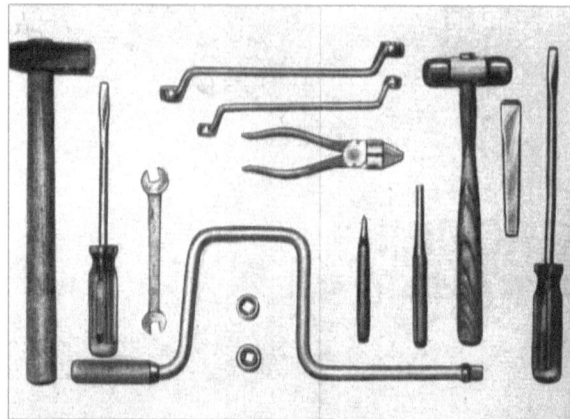

Tools: Open ended spanner 10 mm, ring spanner 9/14 mm, socket spanner 14/17 mm, screwdriver 6/10 mm, hammer, chisel, drift 8 mm, center punch, plastic hammer, T-handle Allen wrench 6 mm.

Fig. 2

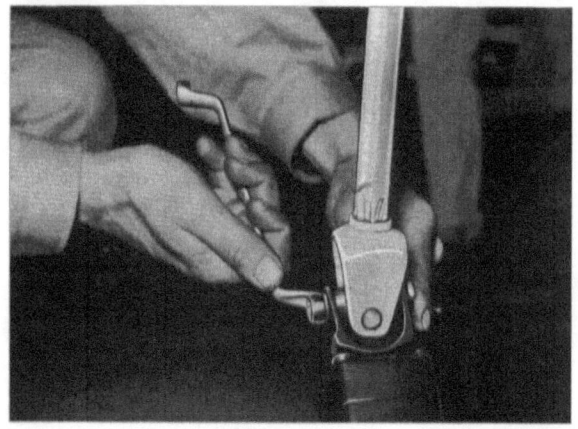

1. Remove split pin from thorough bolt in universal joint and withdraw the bolt. (cotter pin pliers, open ended spanner 10 mm, ring spanner 9 mm)

Fig. 3

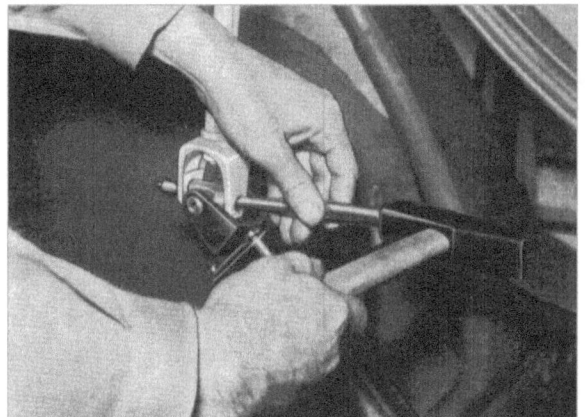

2. Drive cross pin out of universal joint (driver 8 mm, hammer)

Fig. 4

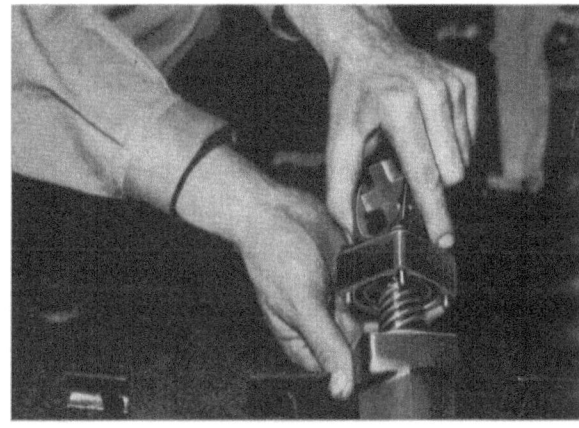

Caution: Pay attention to correct position of the bushings for the thorough bolt. When assembling make certain that the cross pin with the orifice for the thorough bolt is correctly fitted.

3. Protect the door spring shrouding with a cartoon cover to avoid damaging (see Group A Figure 5).

4. Slacken the four slotted-head screws on steering housing and unscrew the steering screw from steering nut by anticlockwise rotation.

Fig. 5

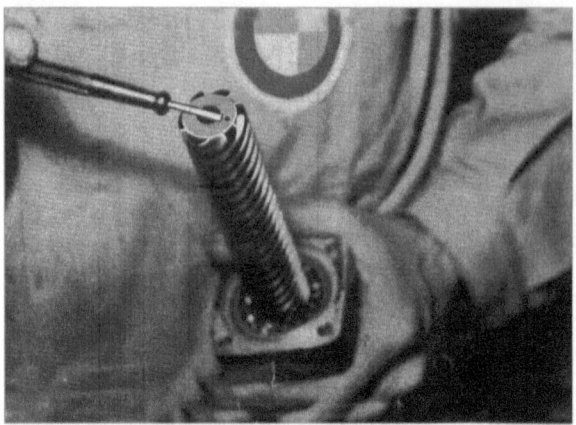

Caution: Steering screw and steering nut are punch-marked. When assembling make sure that the punch-marked spots are fitted together. In case they are not marked at all, mark them on dismantling.

5. Unhook return spring of accelerator pedal from frame tube.

6. Remove cotter pin at linkage end of accelerator pedal and withdraw the linkage rod. (cotter pin pliers)

7. Depress brake pedal, remove split pin and draw out the clevis attaching bolt. (cotter pin pliers)

8. Unhook clutch pedal return spring from the frame.

9. Depress clutch pedal, remove cotter pin, withdraw the clevis bolt. (cotter pin pliers)

10. Detach steering housing from bottom plate. (socket spanner 14 mm with universal joint, on vehicles of recent construction key wrench 6)

11. Press the steering housing slightly rearward and remove it upward. (see also Group A Figure 9)

Fig. 6

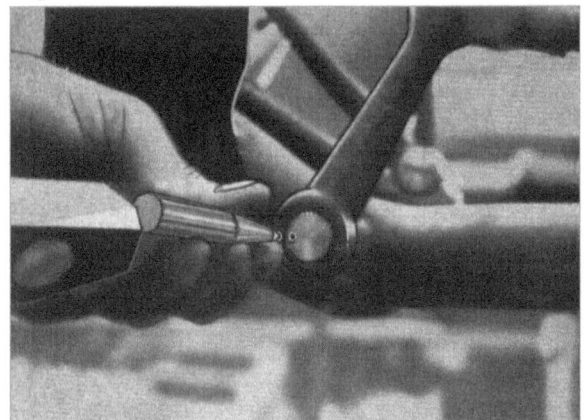

12. Mark the position of steering shaft and steering intermediate arm on outer side of the shaft by means of a center punch.

Fig. 7

13. Slacken steering arm clamping screw, withdraw the steering arm. (ring spanner 14 mm)

14. Slacken three slotted-head screws securing the cover plate to steering housing and remove the plate. (screwdriver 6 mm)

15. Punch-mark steering shaft and steering arm on inner side of the shaft.

Fig. 8

Caution: When installing new parts carry out a basic adjustment of steering, as these parts are not marked (see L10)

16. Slacken clamping screw of steering arm on inner side of steering shaft. (socket spanner 14 mm)

121

Caution: The clamp screw must be fully removed.

17. Drive out steering shaft from inner side outwards, with the aid of a brass driver.

Fig. 9

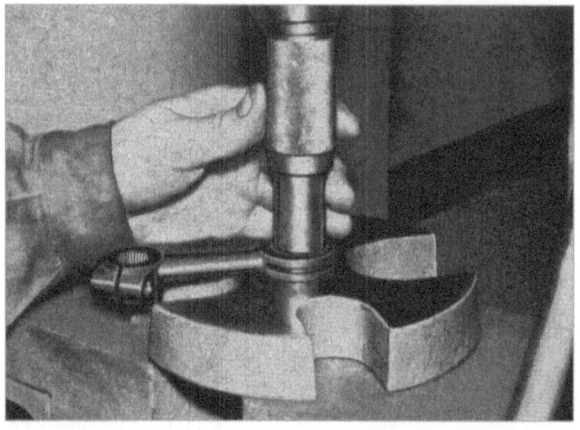

18. Replace the ball bearing in the inner steering arm.

   a) Straighten bent ear of lock washer. (hammer, chisel)

   b) Discard ball bearing and fit a new one with the aid of a press.

Caution: After having pressed in place a new ball bearing clamp the spacer shims again by applying punch blows on the four points indicated on the arm.

Fig. 10

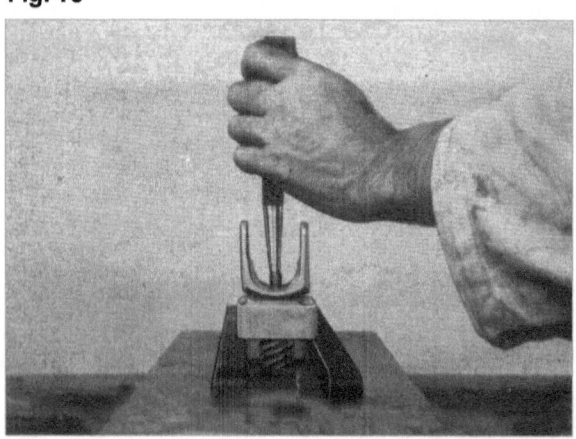

19. Replace ball bearing for the steering screw.

   a) Straighten bent ear of tab washer on steering screw lock nut. (hammer, chisel)

   b) Unscrew the nut on top of steering screw. (socket spanner 17 mm)

   c) Drive steering screw out of universal joint yoke and ball bearing. (punch, hammer)

L2 Removing and refitting steering wheel and steering column

Fig. 11

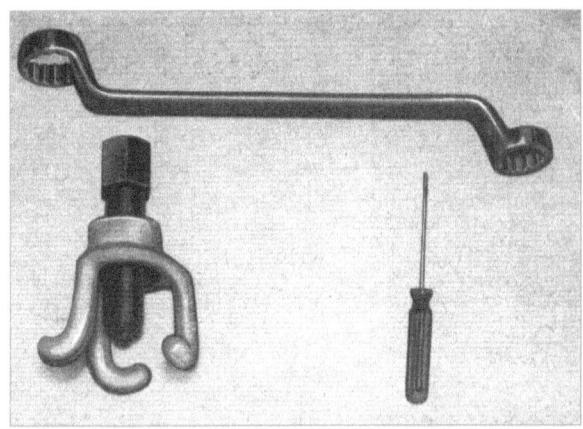

Tools: Steering wheel puller No. 532, ring spanner 32-27 mm, electric screwdriver 2 mm.

Fig. 12

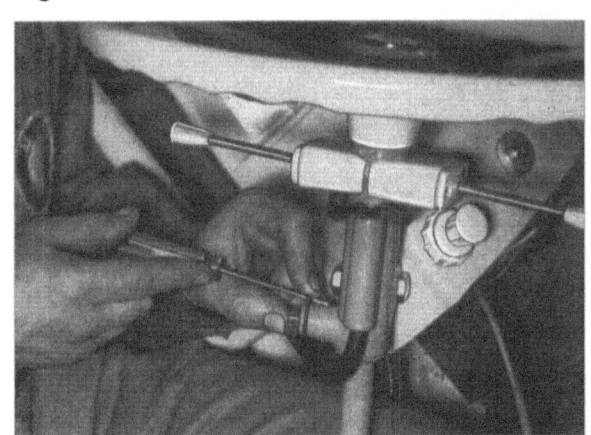

1. Remove snap ring for horn blowing slide contact.

Caution: Hold the snap ring with the finger as otherwise it jumps away.

Fig. 13

2. Grasp horn blowing ring and remove.

Caution: Do not use any tool in order to avoid damaging the horn blowing ring plate or the steering wheel hub. The horn plate can be easily raised with the finger nails.

Fig. 14

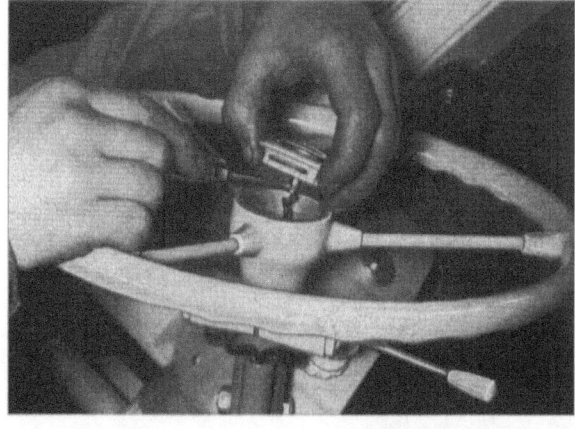

3. Disconnect horn wire from horn blowing ring. (electric screwdriver)

4. Unscrew the steering wheel nut. (ring spanner 27 mm)

Caution: When assembling tighten steering wheel nut only so far as to obtain a play-free movement of the steering assembly.

Fig. 15

5. Attach puller Tool No. 532 and remove steering wheel. (steering wheel puller, ring spanner 32 mm)

6. Remove steering column downwards.

Isetta Factory Repair Manual

Caution: The steering column is mounted on rubber guides that may be withdrawn upwards and downwards by means of two wire hooks. When assembling or fitting new rubber guides insert them with high-pressure grease.

L10 Basic adjustment of steering
("L1 Removing and refitting steering" belongs to this chapter)

Fig. 16

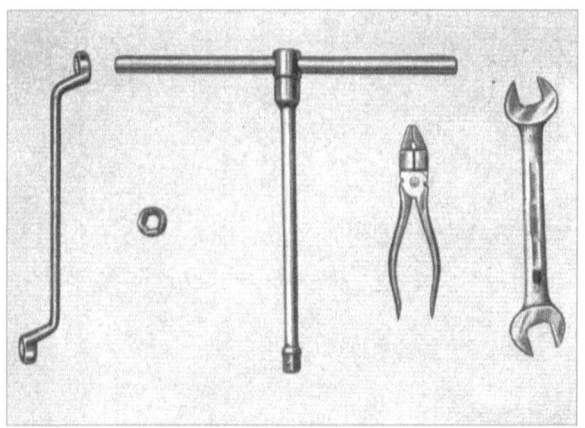

Tools: Open ended spanner 22 mm, socket spanner 14 mm, ring spanner 17 mm, cotter pin pliers.

Fig. 17

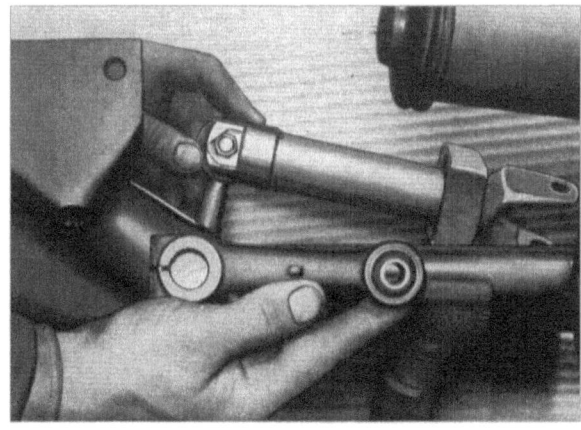

When using new parts adjust steering as follows:

1. Assemble steering shaft and its inner arm.

2. Move inner steering arm rearwards until it abuts on the steering gear housing.

3. Place outer steering arm in position so that it points horizontally – and parallel to the frame – in rearward direction.

125

Fig. 18

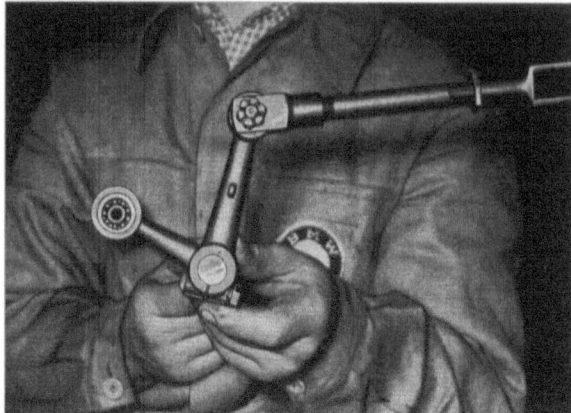

Caution: Then, if the inner steering arm is drawn forwards until it abuts at front, the outer steering arm stands vertically to the chassis.

4. The two steering arms are now situated at the prescribed angle each to other.

Fig. 19

5. In this position tighten the steering arms by means of the clamping screws.

6. Attach steering drag link on the outer steering arm, tighten the nut and repin. (ring spanner 17 mm, cotter pin pliers)

7. Slacken lock nut on the steering drag link. (open ended spanner 22 mm)

Fig 20

8. Place the outer steering arm in central position, that is at an angle of 45 deg. to the chassis.

9. Place the front wheels in straight-ahead position.

10. Rotate clevis unit of steering drag link until the bolt for rear clevis connection goes easily through the steering

knuckle arm. The steering drag link has now a length of 204 mm = 8 inches from eye to eye.

11. Enter the bolt, fit the nut and repin. (ring spanner 17 mm, cotter pin pliers)

12. Tighten lock nut on steering drag link. (open ended spanner 22 mm)

www.VelocePress.com

GROUP F
SPRINGS AND SHOCK ABSORBERS

F1 Removing and refitting front spring

Fig. 1

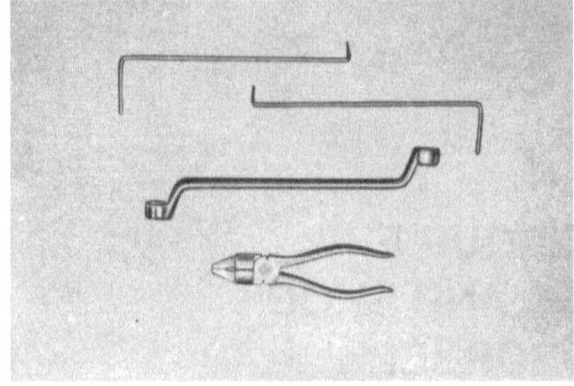

Tools: Ring spanner 17 mm, cotter pin pliers, 2 wire hooks.

1. Support the vehicle discharge the spring.

2. Remove rubber caps.

3. Remove cotter pin from nut securing the pull rod. (cotter pin pliers)

Fig. 2

4. Unscrew the pull rod nut. (ring spanner 17 mm)

Isetta Factory Repair Manual

Fig. 3

5. Remove cover plate and coil spring, draw out the two rubber bumpers with the aid of the two wire hooks.

Fig. 4

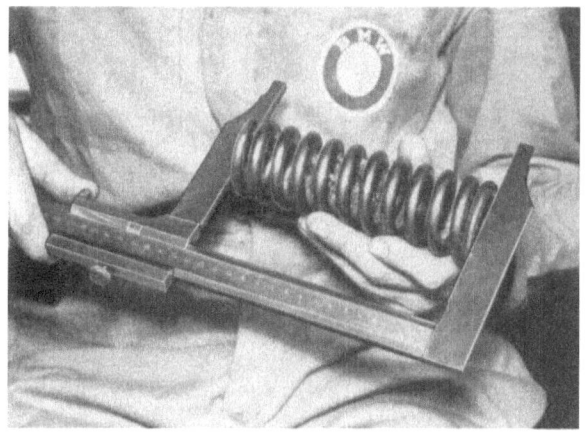

6. Check the length of the spring.

Caution: The unloaded spring length should be 170 mm = 6.8 inches.

Fig. 5

7. When refitting, grease the front spring.

Order of refitting:

Rubber bumper
Rubber bumper
Coil spring
Cover plate

8. Place the nut in position, tighten and repin.

Caution: The coil spring has the right amount of initial tension, if the cotter pin hole machined through the pull rod is clearly visible in the castellated nut.

9. Replace the rubber cap.

F5 Replacing friction disc

Fig. 6

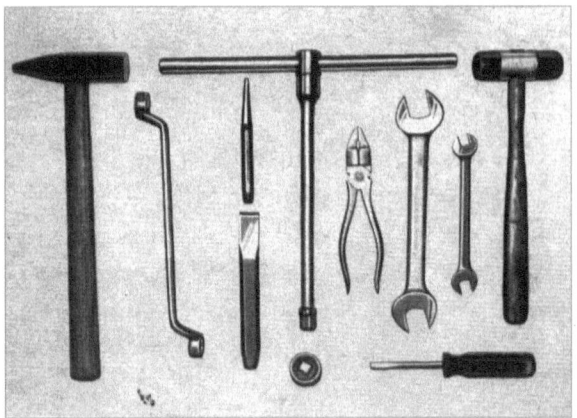

Tools: Ring spanner 17 mm, open ended spanner 10/22 mm, wheel nut spanner, hammer, chisel, brass drift, plastic hammer, cotter pin pliers, screwdriver.

Fig. 7

1. Remove wheel cover plate, slacken wheel nuts, supporting the vehicle and remove the wheel.

2. Slacken the nut fixing the shaft of spring pullrod. (ring spanner 17 mm)

3. Drive out spring rod shaft by means of a plastic hammer, or with a brass drift, if very tight. (plastic hammer, hammer, brass drift)

Fig. 8

4. Straighten tab washer for screw on swing arms shaft. (chisel, hammer)

5. Slacken screw on swing arm shaft. (open ended spanner 22 mm)

Fig. 9

6. Remove swing arm together with the brake plate.

7. Remove the damper plate on inner side of steering knuckle. (open ended spanner 10 mm)

Caution: When assembling tighten the screw only after having centered the damper plate with the friction disc.

8. Check the length of damper plate springs. Length of unloaded springs should be 34 mm (1 1/3").

Caution: When assembling make certain that the rubber washer seats correctly between the friction disc and damper plate,

Fig. 10

and that the damper plate seats with its hole upon the locating pin on swing arm.

The reassembly is carried out in exactly the reverse order. When assembling grease the damper plate a little bit in order to avoid its blocking.

F10 Removing and refitting a rear spring

Fig. 11

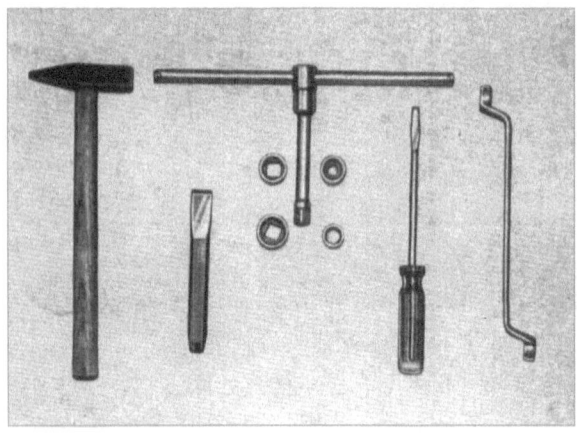

Tools: Screwdriver, wheel nut spanner, box spanners 14/17/19 mm, ring spanner 17 mm, hammer, chisel.

1. Remove wheel cover plate, slacken wheel nuts, support the vehicle at rear, locating the support beneath the cross member.

2. Remove the wheel.

3. Straighten the tab washer for the nut of spring-leaf retainer. (hammer, chisel)

Isetta Factory Repair Manual

Fig. 12

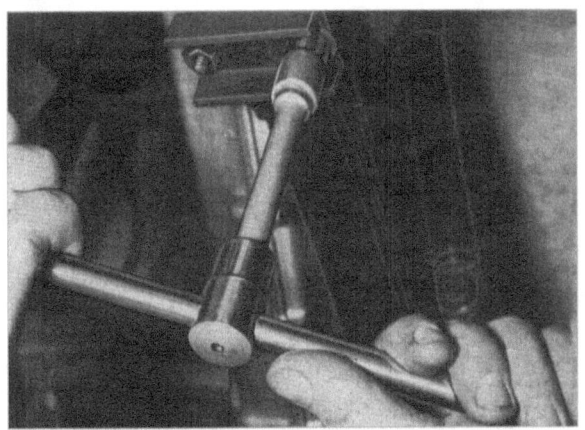

4. Unscrew the nut of spring-leaf retainer. (box spanner 14 mm)

Fig. 13

5. Slacken nut of spring-eye bolt, withdraw the bolt downwards. (box spanner 17 mm, ring spanner 17 mm)

Fig. 14

6. Unscrew the bolt fixing rear end of spring to back axle housing. (box spanner 19 mm)

Caution: This bolt on the left-hand side must not be tightened with extreme force, tighten it only until it is right home, for otherwise the thread would be torn out of the aluminum casing.

Fig. 15

Caution: The right-hand side of this bolt features a nut.

7. Withdraw the leaf spring rearwards and downwards.

The reassembly is carried in exactly the reverse order.

F15 Removing and refitting shock absorber at rear

Fig. 16

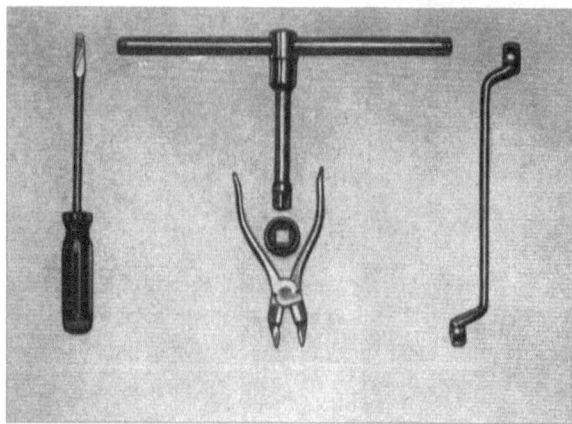

Tools: Screwdriver, wheel nut spanner, ring spanner 17 mm, open ended spanner 17 mm, cotter pin pliers.

1. Remove wheel cover plate, slacken wheel nuts, support the vehicle below the cross member.

2. Remove the wheel.

Isetta Factory Repair Manual

Fig. 17

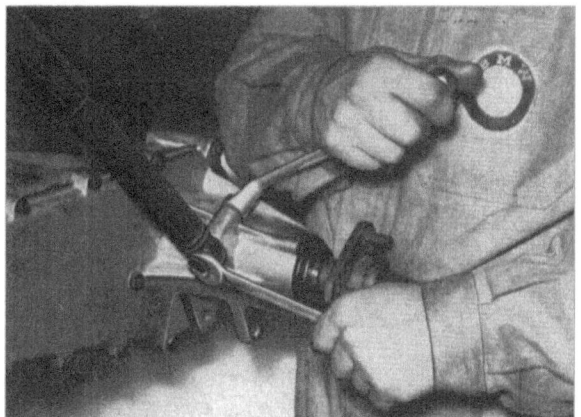

3. Remove cotter pin from nut of shock absorber lower fixing bolt and slacken the nut. (cotter pin pliers 17 mm, open ended spanner 17 mm)

4. Press out the lower fixing bolt.

Fig. 18

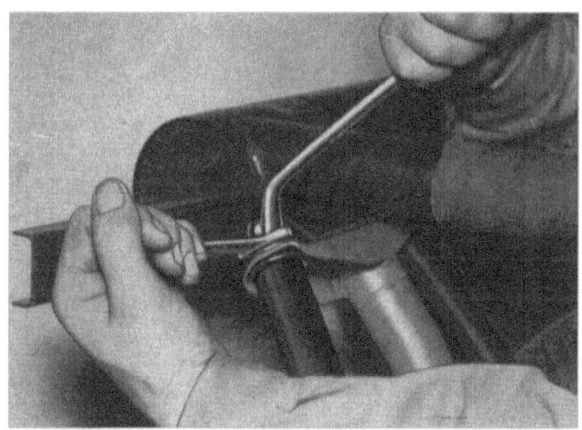

5. Slacken lock nut and nut of shock absorber top fixation. (open ended spanner 17 mm, ring spanner 17 mm)

Fig. 19

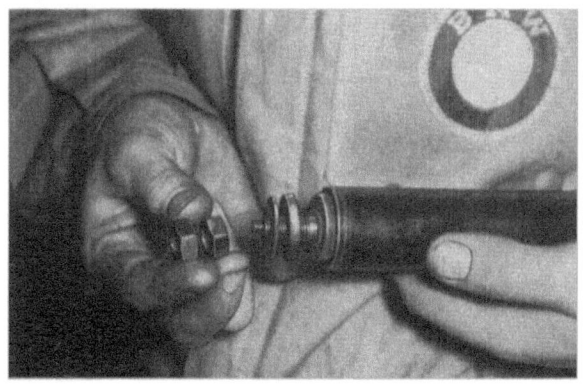

6. Withdraw shock absorber downwards.

Caution: When assembling remember correct order of top fixation components: Rubber ring – shock absorber support – rubber ring – washer – nut – nut.

Fig. 20

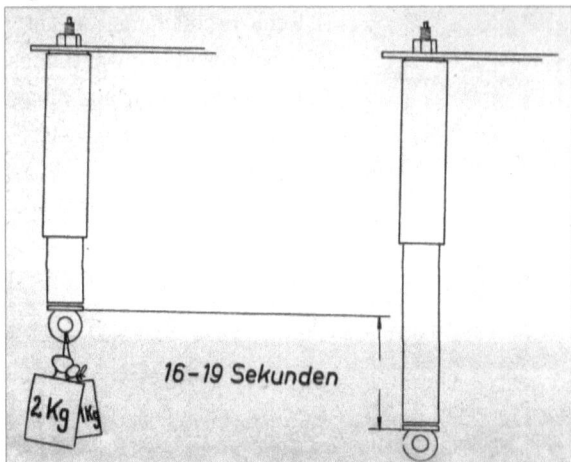

Caution: To check the shock absorber proceed as follows: Fix shock absorber to a flat steel plate, attach a weight of 3 kg (6.6 lbs). Shock absorber must slide downwards in 16 to 19 seconds.

GROUP B
BRAKES, WHEELS, TIRES

B1 Adjusting brakes

Fig. 1

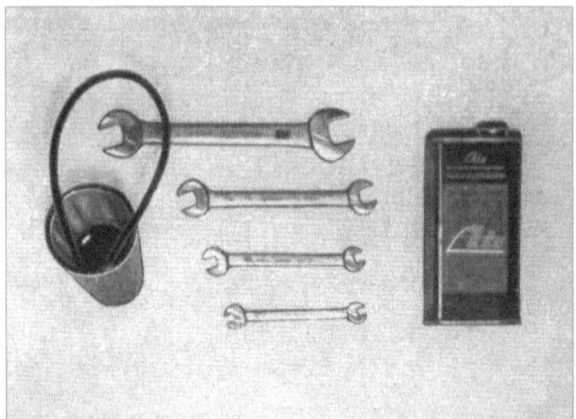

Tools: Open ended spanner 7/8/12/19 mm, ATE brake fluid, glass jar, rubber bleed tube.

Fig. 2

Caution: The rear brake should be adjusted somewhat lighter in order to ensure even braking on all four wheels.

1. Support the vehicle so that all four wheels are clear of the ground.

2. Bleed the three wheel cylinders.

a) Remove rubber cover from the bleeder nipple and attach the bleeder hose.

b) Place other end of hose in a glass jar half full of ATE blue brake fluid, as shown in figure 2.

c) Open bleeder valve ½ turn. (open ended spanner 7 mm)

Fig. 3

d) Operate brake pedal slowly until fluid runs out of bleeder hose in a solid stream without air bubbles.

e) After expelling all traces of air, hold brake pedal in depressed position, tighten nipple and replace rubber dust excluder.

Caution: During the bleeding care should be taken to see that the reservoir is replenished frequently in order to keep the master cylinder filled while bleeding the brake system.

Fig. 4

Bleeding order:
    Rear right
    Front right
    Front left.

3. On all three brakes successively slacken

a) lock nut on eccentric (cam). (open ended spanner 19 mm)

b) adjust square-headed screw in a clockwise direction, at the same time rotating the wheel in driving direction until a light drag is noted. (open ended spanner 8 mm)

c) Then back off the adjusting screw until the wheel just turns freely. In this position secure the adjuster with the lock nut.

Fig. 5

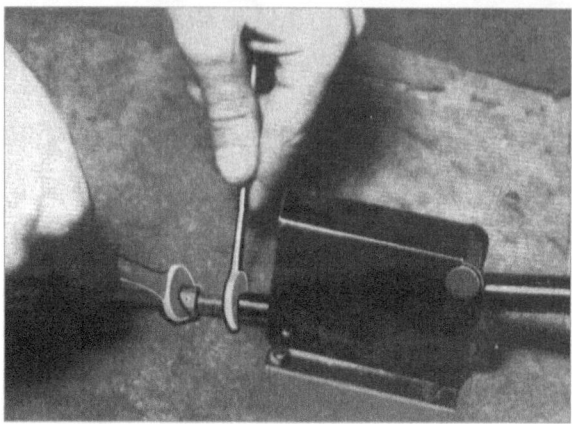

4. To adjust the hand brake slacken the lock nut on adjusting screw. (open ended spanner 12 mm)

5. Tighten the adjusting screw in an anticlockwise direction until the rear brake just begins to rub. Then return until the rear wheels run freely and one turn more.

6. Tighten lock nut.

B10 Relining brakes

Fig. 6

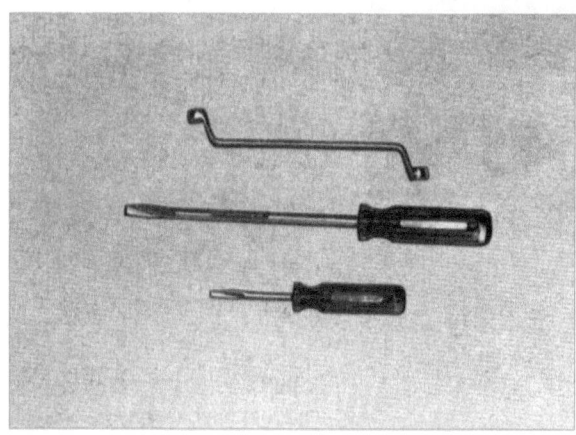

Tools: Screwdriver 6/12 mm, ring spanner 10 mm.

1. Remove wheel cover plate, slacken wheel nuts, support the vehicle.

2. Remove the wheel, remove brake drum.

Fig. 7

3. With the aid of screwdrivers press the brake shoes away from wheel cylinder and eccentric. (2 screwdrivers)

Fig. 8

4. With the quadrangular hub flange in a convenient position, press the brake shoes on their inner side outwards, support them upon the hub flange, tilt and remove the brake shoes.

Fig. 9

Caution: When assembling front brakes be sure the brake shoes are fitted in correct position. The flat head slotted screw for the anchor plate must register with the big hole machined in the brake shoe.

5. Having exchanged the brake shoes carry out the reassembly in exactly the reverse order.

Fig. 10

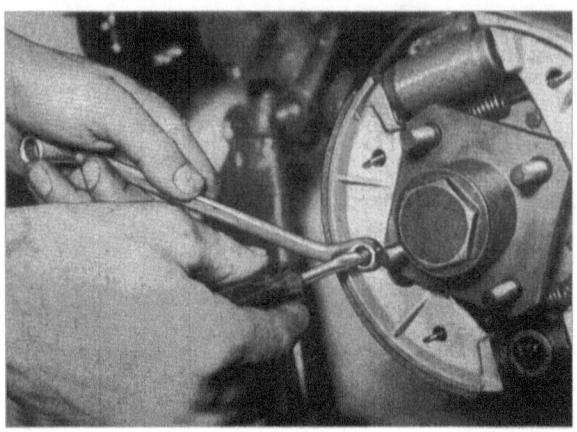

6. After having installed new brake shoes set them at an equal distance to the anchor plate by operating the adjusting screw accordingly. (small screwdriver, ring spanner 10 mm)

Caution: If a brake shoe results misaligned after a short test braking (uneven wear), it will also be aligned by means of the adjusting screw, so that it fits squarely with the drum. To overhaul the rear brake it is necessary to remove the wheel hub with the brake drum. To carry out the further jobs proceed in accordance with the above indications.

The reassembly is made in reverse order.

B13 Adjusting master cylinder

Fig. 11

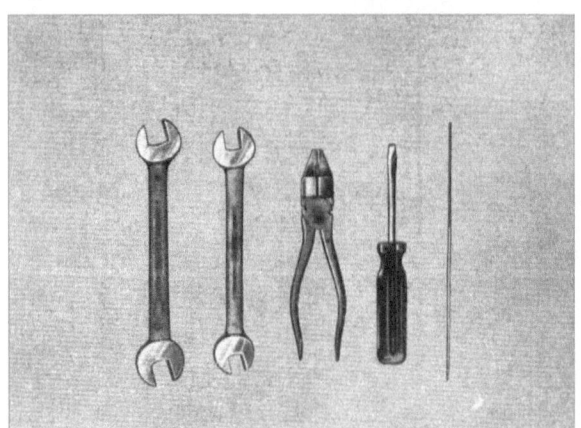

Tools: Cotter pin pliers, open ended spanner 14/17 mm, screwdriver, wire 1 mm ∅

Isetta Factory Repair Manual

Fig. 12

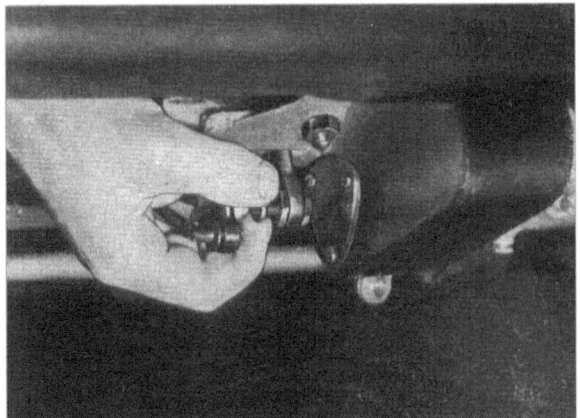

1. Remove cotter pin from brake rod securing bolt on pedal end. (cotter pin pliers)

2. Remove brake rod bolt.

Fig. 13

3. Slacken lock nut on adjusting nut. (open ended spanner 14 mm, hold brake rod with a 17 mm spanner)

Fig. 14

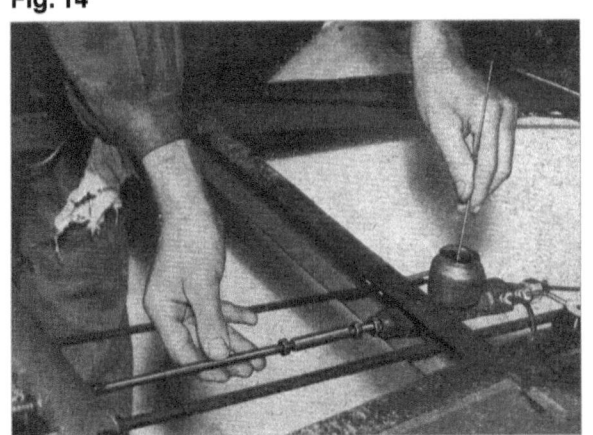

4. Push in the brake rod and at the same time touch the compensating bore in bottom of mater cylinder with the aid of a wire stick (1 mm). Slide the piston until it abuts on the wire.

Caution: If with the brake pedal in normal position the compensating bore is not free, the stop light lights continually, because the pressure lasts upon the stop light switch.

5. In the found position rotate brake rod until the bolt may be easily slid through clevis and break pedal.

Fig. 15

6. Locate adjusting nut in center position between the two brake rod halves and secure by means of the two 14 mm lock nuts. (open ended spanner 14 mm and open ended spanner 17 mm)

Caution: As of chassis No. 404 360 the adjusting nut features a right-and-left-handed thread that obviates the necessity of detaching the brake rod in order to adjust the brake. Jobs 1 and 2 are superseded by virtue of this modification.

B20 Tire fitting
(To fit the split-rim wheel no tire levers are required)

Fig. 16

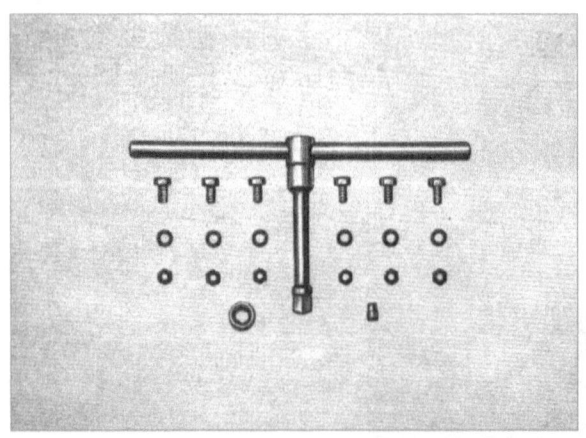

Tools: Socket spanner 14 mm.

1. Inflate the tube sufficiently to round it out.

Isetta Factory Repair Manual

Fig. 17

2. Rub tire with talcum.

3. Slip tube into the cover.

Fig. 18

4. Insert inner ring so that the cranked valve points outwards.

Fig. 19

5. Now locate the outer plate so that the cranked valve fits through the hole.

6. Align inner ring with respect to the outer plate.

147

Fig. 20

7. Connect inner ring to outer plate by means of bolts, circlips and nuts, the threaded ends of bolts pointing outwards.

8. Tighten bolts firmly in diagonal order.

9. Inflate tires to 14 lbs./sq. in. at rear, and 17 lbs./sq. in. at front and spare wheel.

GROUP A
BODY

A1   Removing and refitting body

Fig. 1

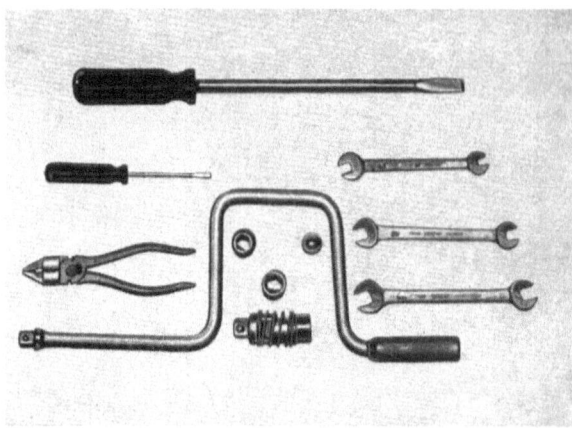

Tools: Socket spanner 9/10/14 mm with universal joint, open ended spanner 7/9/12/13 mm, cotter pin pliers, electric screwdriver 8 mm, T-handle Allan wrench 6 mm.

Caution: On the vehicles of recent construction it is necessary to slacken the two body fixing screws in the corners at left and right as well as the four screws securing the steering gear housing (see job 14), the width of 8 mm of hollow center of which requires a 6 mm plug wrench.

A) Jobs to be carried out within the body

Fig. 2

1. Remove covering board below the seat, spare wheel and seat, remove rubber floor mat, and shut the fuel tap.

2. Dismount battery, disconnect negative cable from floor board (socket spanner 10 mm). Detach positive cable from battery (open ended spanner 13 mm).

Caution: The screw securing earth (ground) connection serves also as body fixation.

3. Slacken 7 body fixing screws. (socket spanner 10 mm)

Isetta Factory Repair Manual

Fig. 3

4. Slacken the two body securing screws at front, right and left. (socket spanner 14 mm)

5. Detach the support of hand brake lever, by removing four screws. (socket spanner 9 mm)

6. Remove cotter pin from handbrake lever pin, withdraw the lever pin. (cotter pin pliers)

Fig. 4

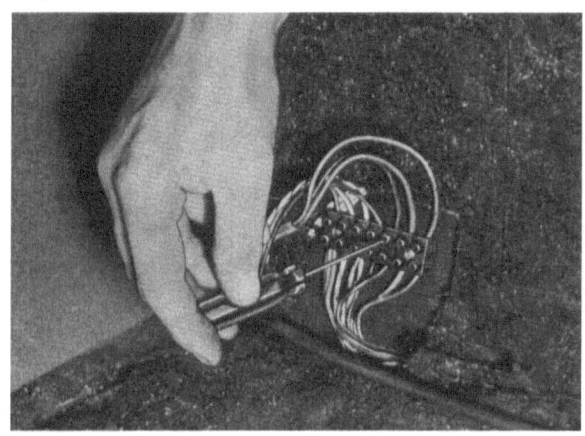

7. Slacken adjusting nut for hand brake, lift out the cable, remove slotted bolt and push cable through in rearward direction. (open ended spanner 12mm)

Caution: Make certain not to lose the rubber grommet.

8. Remove rubber sealing on the liquid reservoir of brake master cylinder (screwdriver)

9. Disconnect three wires from cable connector unit, green – blue – red/black. (electric screwdriver)

Fig. 5

10. Protect the doors spring shroud with a cartoon cover to prevent its damaging.

Fig. 6

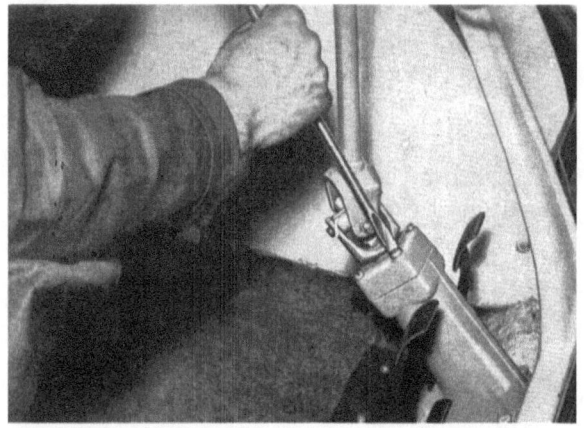

11. Slacken four slotted screws on top of steering gear housing. (screwdriver 8 mm)

Fig. 7

12. Turn steering screw out of steering nut by rotating steering wheel in an anticlockwise direction.

Isetta Factory Repair Manual

Caution: Guide the steering column with the hand, so that the steering screw leaves the housing vertically.

Fig. 8

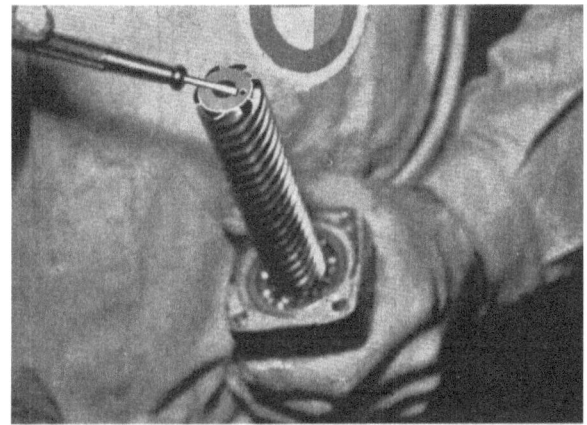

13. Envelop the steering screw with a clean cloth.

Caution: When assembling make sure that the punch mark on the steering screw registers with the correspondent mark on steering nut, eventually mark steering screw and nut together.

14. Slacken four screws fixing steering gear housing to the floor board. (socket spanner 14 mm, on vehicles of recent construction use plug wrench 6 mm)

Caution: The steering gear housing cannot be lifted unless job 15 and the following ones have been carried out.

B) Jobs to be carried out on the vehicle's underside at front

Fig. 9

15. Unhook accelerator pedal return spring on frame tube.

16. Remove cotter pin on accelerator pedal and push out the linkage. (cotter pin pliers)

17. Depress brake pedal, remove cotter pin from clevis pin and withdraw the latter. (cotter pin pliers)

18. Unhook clutch return spring on frame.

19. Depress clutch pedal, remove cotter pin and the linkage. (cotter pin pliers)

20. Disconnect horn wire from the electric horn.

21. Press steering gear housing slightly rearwards and remove upwards.

C) Jobs to be carried out on engine side

22. remove engine covering panel.

23. Draw the three disconnected wires, green, blue, red/black, out of the body. (see job 9)

Fig. 10

24. Disconnect starter cable from engine. (open ended spanner 7 mm)

25. Withdraw petrol (gasoline) rubber hose from carburetor.

26. Bend up the sheet metal clip holding choke and accelerator (throttle) cables

27. Disengage choke operating cable upon having pushed back the rubber grommet, and draw same out together with the choke piston. (open ended spanner 11 mm)

Isetta Factory Repair Manual

Fig. 11

28. Slacken the two body fixing bolts upon the engine carrying chassis member. (socket spanner 10 mm and open ended spanner 10 mm)

D) Jobs to be carried out on the side opposite to engine

Fig. 12

29. Remove both transverse gear control rods from the selector mechanism by removing cotter and clevis pins.

30. Remove speedometer (flexible drive) cable from chain case by unscrewing the union nut.

31. Push rubber hose connecting air intake arrangement to air silencer towards the latter.

32. Disconnect the cable leading to the stop light switch. (electric screwdriver)

Fig. 13

33. Lift the body with three men. Two men grasp the body on the front fenders, one man on rear bumper. The stern of the body must be raised sufficiently high in order to get it clear over the engine top.

Fig. 14

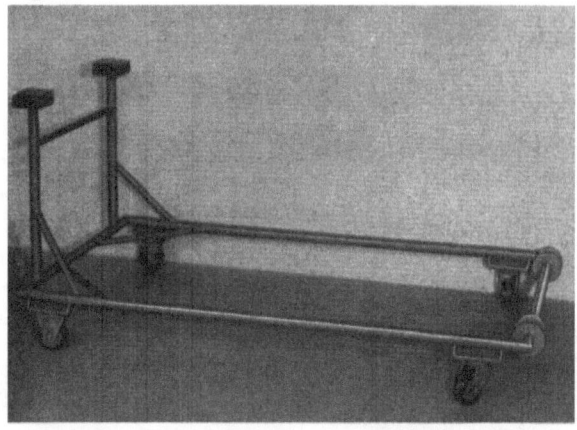

Fig. 15

34. Place the body upon a special support stand mounted on rolls as shown in Figure 14.

To carry out the reassembly proceed in exactly the reverse order.

A 5 Replacing a glass panel

Fig. 16

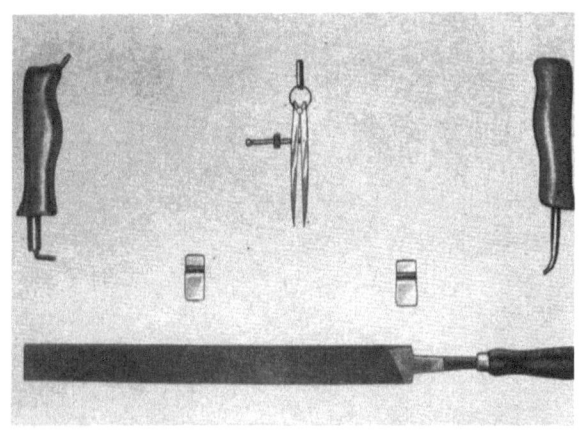

Tools: Bastard file, scriber, special tool for glass installation, special weatherstrip retainer tool, divider, two clips to hold the glass for tracing contours.

The window glass to be replaced is removed by carefully pulling retainer from weatherstrip and pushing out the glass panel. The weatherstrip will stay in place in the body opening, from where it is easily removed.

1. Locate the new glass panel on the body opening with the aid of fixing clips. (two fixing clips)

Fig. 17

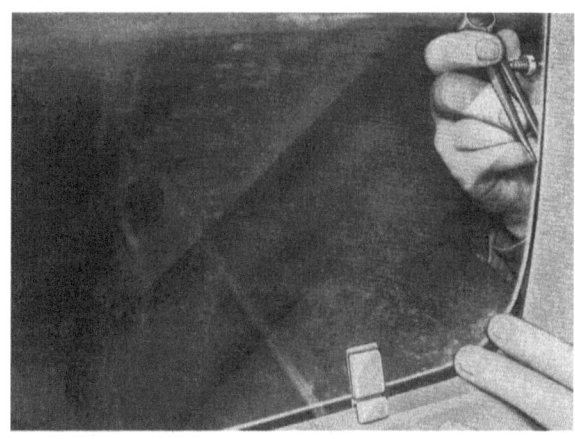

2. With the above divider circle trace a line upon the plexiglass pane at a distance of 9 mm from the body border.

3. Using the bastard file cut the plexiglass panel along the traced line.

Fig. 18

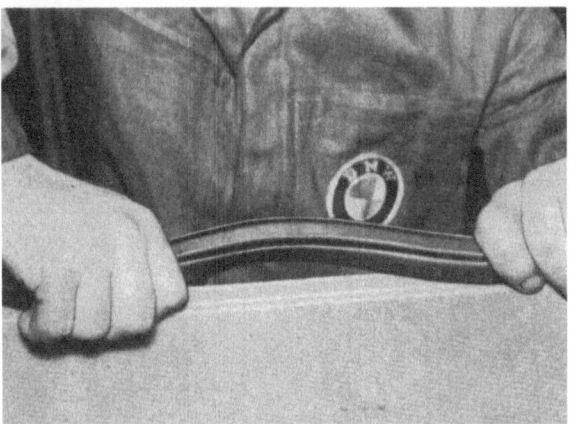

4. Push in place the weatherstrip all around the body opening.

Fig. 19

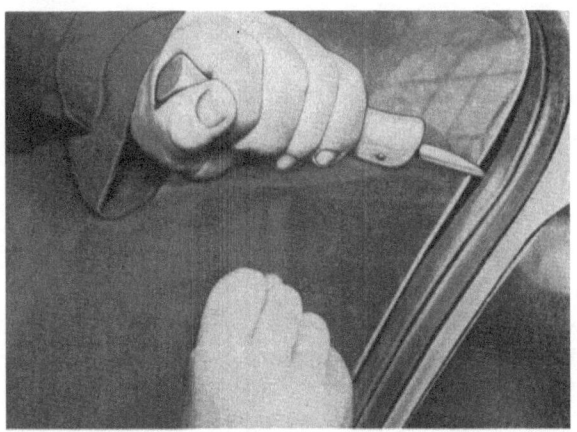

5. Locate the glass over the opening and pushing down the glass slide it into the glass groove of the weatherstrip. Use the above special tool to force the lip of the weatherstrip over the glass around its entire circumference. Use cement Terokal B to bond the weatherstrip at the joint edges in order to prevent entry of water.

Fig. 20

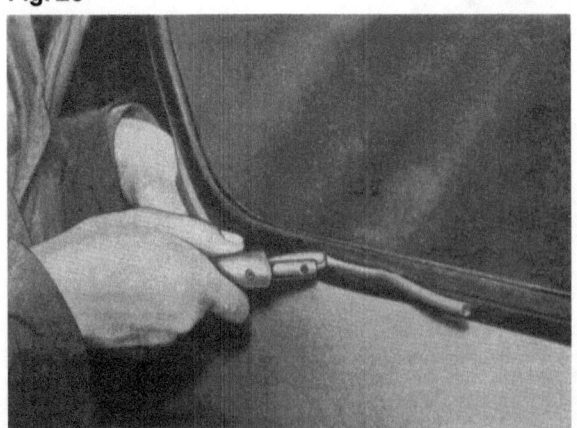

6. Thread retainer (locking strip) in retainer installing tool and pulling same enter retainer in the corresponding groove all around the weatherstrip.

7. Cut the retainer ends in order to obtain a proper joint and push them down into the weatherstrip.

Caution: The joint of the two retainer ends must always be on the lower side of the glass panel.

www.VelocePress.com

GROUP R
CHASSIS FRAME

R1 Measuring frame after an accident

Fig. 1

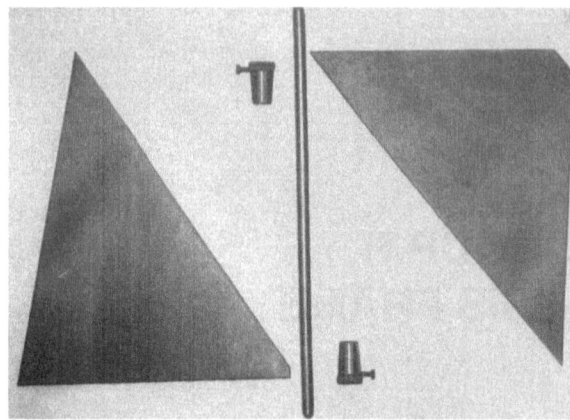

Includes the following jobs. A1, M2, L1, H1, V1.

Tools: Test arbour with insert cones, gauge for checking castor angle, gauge for checking king pin inclination and camber.

Fig. 2

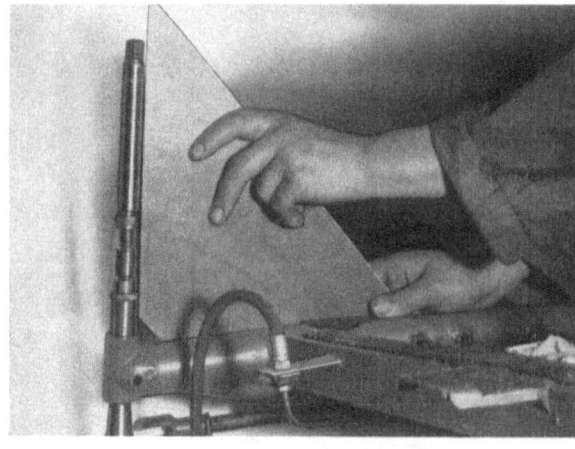

To check a frame for correct alignment it must be completely free. As measuring points serve:

1. Steering knuckle king pin bearing.

2. Holes in rear cross member for eye bolts of cantilever springs.

Since nearly all frontal accidents cause the bending of the short tube ends bearing the front suspension assemblies, these must first be checked for correct castor and toe position. This is made with the aid of triangular sheet metal gauges specially developed for this purpose.

To checking pin inclination and camber, jam test arbour with the two cones in the bearing hold for steering knuckle king pin, place the gauge upon the cross tube and approach it to the test arbour until a visual test may be made. To do this make certain that the gauge applies evenly along the tube and remove body damping strips which might hinder this operation.

Fig. 3

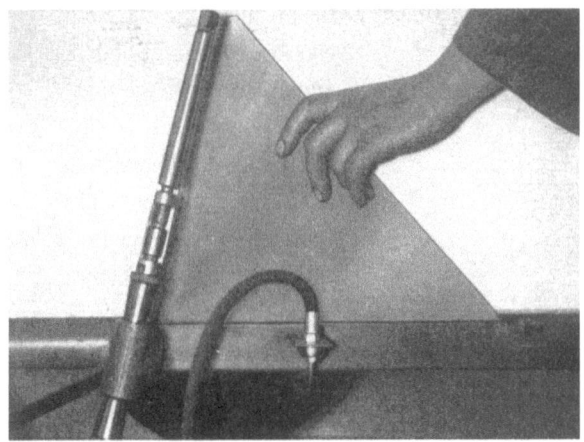

In the same manner check the castor angle. For this purpose place the gauge upon the box-section side member behind the cross tube carrying the front suspension and push it ahead until a visual test may be made.

The frame tube end for reception of steering knuckle king pin can after light accidents be straightened in cold condition, and in warm condition if the bent is due to a serious accident.

Fig. 4

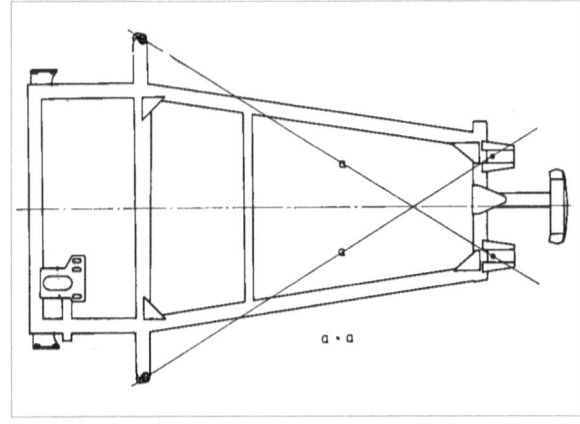

Furthermore the frame must be checked for distortion that may occur if the blow hit the vehicle on a front corner. For this ascertain the center line of frame by measuring and determine same by a well stretched steel wire. Then perform a diagonal measurement from king pin bearing hole to opposite cantilever spring eye-bolt hole. The two measuring lines must meet each other upon the center line determined by a wire and may differ by a maximum of 3 mm in the length. This diagonal measurement greatly amplifies an eventual distortion, so that it is easily recognized.

Fig. 5

Finally the frame may be checked for distortion by aiming over from the side.

If a frame is badly distorted due to a serious accident and cannot be straightened in cold condition, it should be replaced.

Fig. 5

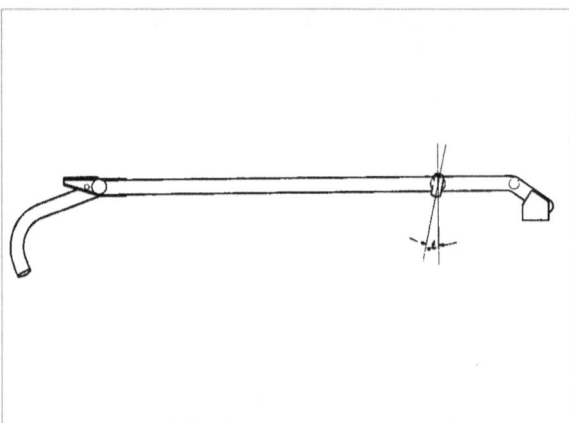

Finally the frame may be checked for distortion by aiming over from the side.

If a frame is badly distorted due to a serious accident and cannot be straightened in cold condition, it should be replaced.

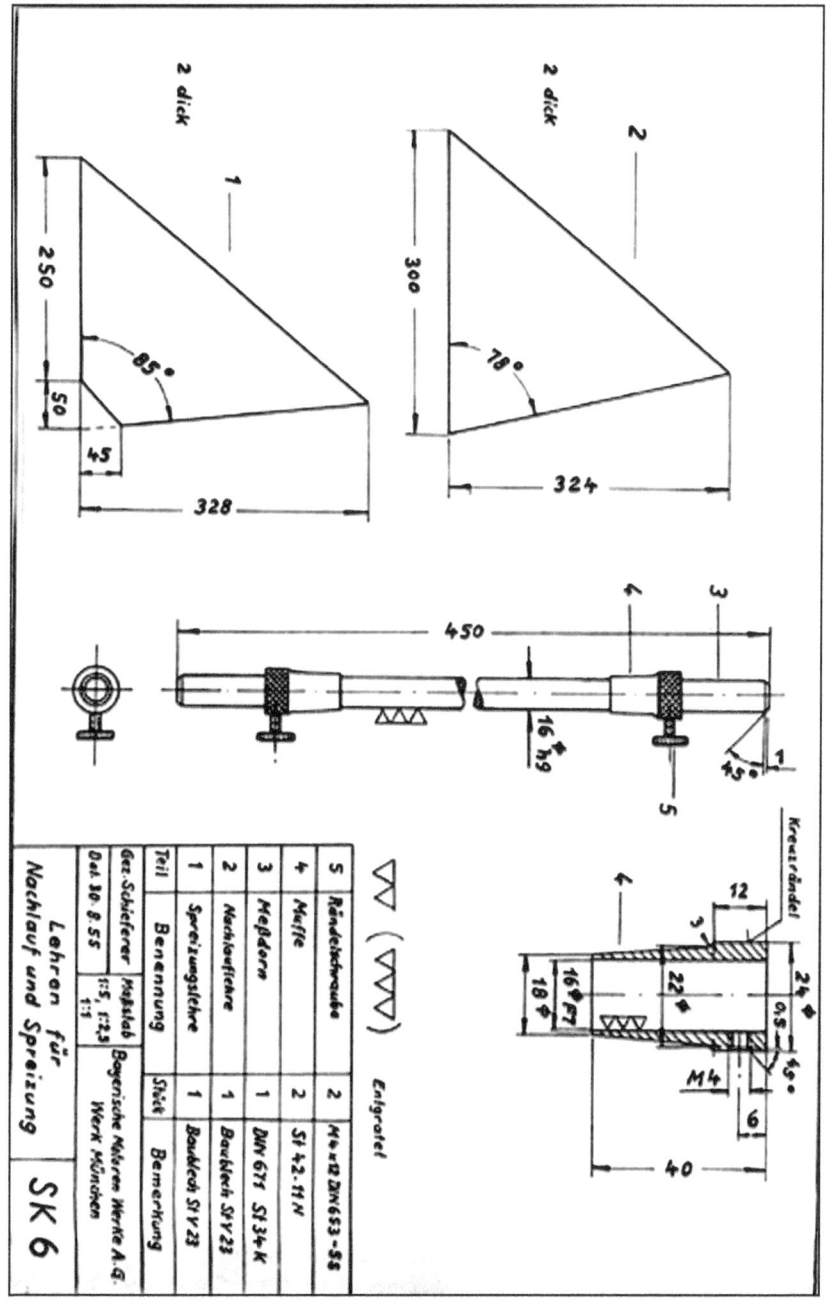

www.VelocePress.com

GROUP E
ELECTRICAL SYSTEM

Description of the electrical system
(see wiring diagram)

The electrical equipment consists of the following components:

A) Components fitted to engine

1. Noris dynamo starter, on front extension of crankshaft with two separate field coil assemblies (for starter and dynamo) and blower wheel with cam ring and automatic advance unit. The contact breaker sits on dynamo front plate, easily accessible for adjustment through holes in blower wheel. The whole assembly is fitted to the timing case cover by means of 4 screws and protected by a front-end cover upon the blower wheel.

The connections for starter and dynamo pass through a rubber-garnished lateral opening in the blower wheel housing. The various leads are assembled in one wiring harness and identified by the following colours:

    a) blue lead 91[+]: From positive carbon brush of dynamo to cable connector unit II/2.

    b) black-red lead 92: From dynamo field coil assembly to cable connector unit II/3.

    c) black lead 93: From contact breaker to terminal 1 of ignition coil.

    d) green lead 90 does not come out of the dynamo starter, but runs directly from cable connector unit II/1 to terminal 15 of ignition coil.

To the dynamo starter pertains the cut-out and regulator unit with starter relay, which is – for the sake of protection – situated behind the battery inside the vehicle. Voltage regulator (same type as used for motorcycle) and cut-out relay are mounted upon a common base plate and protected by a sheet metal cover. The field resistor is fitted to the bottom side of the base plate, that features five terminals.

[+] *The lead numbers correspond with the cable designations in annexed wiring diagram.*

Isetta Factory Repair Manual

Terminal A for main lead to starter

Terminal 51/30 for cable to positive terminal of battery

Terminal 50 to terminal 50 of starter switch in instrument panel

Terminal 61/D+ for connection of lead 4 to cable connector unit I/11 and

Lead 18 to cable connector unit II/2

Terminal DF for connection of lead 19 to cable connector unit II/3.

The electrical load of starter is:

a) start, about 9 Amps

b) finish, about 35 to 40 Amps.

The dynamo (generator) has a rated output of 90 Amps and it may be run with a maximum of 130 Amps. To adjust the voltage regulator of generator observe the following values:

Slow-running tension: 14.4 to 14.8 Volts,

tension with rated output of 90 Watts: 12.5 to 13 Volts.

Make certain that the earth (ground) connection of regulator is always in proper condition.

2. Noris ignition coil with condenser, fixed to timing case cover by means of a bracket. For connections see point 1.

Setting timing: This job requires a 12V test lamp, a breaker point gauge 0.4 mm and a screwdriver.

The adjustment is made according to M 30.

B) Components fitted to chassis frame

1. Noris electrical horn, mounted beneath the bumper before front wheel and connected by leads 30 and 31 to cable connector units I/1 and I/2, respectively.

2. Stop light switch is fitted to master cylinder of brake system and connected by leads 12 and 13 to connector units II/1 and II/4 respectively.

C) Components fitted to body

1. Battery 6V/31 Amp. hours, is located beneath the seat. Behind it is the cut-out and regular unit, as already mentioned under A. As usual it has shunt connection to dynamo and is linked with the current consuming units via regulator terminal 51/30 and lead 2 to connector unit I/13.

2. The instrument panel is main switching board contains:

a) the ignition and starter switch with terminals 30, 50, and 15/54. Terminal 30 is connected by lead 62 to cable connector unit I/13 and then by cable 2 to battery and generator. Rotation of ignition key connects terminals 15/54 and 50 to terminal 30.

Switch positions: First stop: Ignition and daytime consumers; pushing-in the key and further rotation operates the starter through the starter relay.

b) Six-pole fuse box with fuses 1 to 6.

> The following consumers are connected:
>
> To fuse 1: Long beam light of left-hand headlamp.
>
> To fuse 2: Long beam light of right-hand headlamp and headlamp main beam control light.
>
> To fuse 3: Dipped beam light for both headlamps.
>
> To fuse 4: Tail lamp left and parking light of both headlamps.
>
> To fuse 5: Tail lamp right and speedometer light.
>
> To fuse 6: Electric horn, screen wiper motor, directional flasher and stop light switch.

c) Lighting switch with terminals 30, 56 and 58. Terminal 30 is connected by lead 71 to terminal 30 of ignition and starter switch. Clockwise rotation of knob to first stop switches on parking and license plate lights and the tail lights, turning to second stop cuts-in the headlamps.

d) Directional flasher with terminals 15, 54 and K. With ignition being switched-on the terminals 54 and 15 receive electrical load via fuse 6 and lead 76. Terminal 54 is connected by lead 78 to identical terminal of directional flasher on steering column guide. From terminal K the lead 77 is taken to direction indicator control light. Lead 63 (general earth (ground) lead) is attached by a lid clip beneath the directional flasher.

e) The two-pole ignition control light is connected with one pole to terminal 15/54 of ignition and starter switch, via lead 79, and the other pole to cable connector unit I/11, via lead 60, and then by lead 4 to terminal 61 /D+ of cut-out and regulator unit.

f) The direction indicator control light is connected by positive pole to terminal K of directional flasher, via lead 77. The lamp nacelle has earth (ground) connection.

g) The headlamp main beam control light is connected by positive pole to fuse 2, via lead 80, and then by lead 73 to terminal 56a of headlamp dipper switch. The nacelle has earth (ground) connection. All three lights before mentioned are equipped with a 12V/2W lamp.

h) The speedometer with flexible drive shaft. Speedometer light is connected by lead 82 to fuse 5.

3. The electrical components fitted to steering column guide:

a) The horn blowing slide contact is connected by lead 56 to connector unit I/2, and then by lead 31 to negative pole of electric hole. The steering column carries an insulated contact ring, upon which slides the contact carbon. The contact ring is connected by a cable to the horn button on steering wheel and by pushing same the earth (ground) connection is obtained.

b) The headlamp dipper switch with terminals 56, 56a and 56b is located on the left-hand side of steering column guide. Terminal 56 is connected by lead 72 to terminal 56 of lighting switch, terminal 56a by lead 73 to fuse 1 and 2 (headlamp long beam lights) and terminal 56b by lead 74 to fuse 3 (headlamp dipped beam lights).

c) The directional signal switch with terminals 54, L, R is fitted to the right-hand side of steering column guide. Terminal 54 is connected to identical terminal of directional flasher, whereas from terminal 1 ble connector unit I/8 and the connector unit I/8 and then by lead 7 to positive pole to left-hand directional signal light. Terminal R is connected by lead 58 to cable connector unit I/9 and then by lead 6 to positive pole of right-hand directional signal light.

4. The headlamps are situated upon the front wheel mudguards, right and left. To the left-hand headlamp lead the cables 32 (dipped beam light), 33 (long beam light), 34 (parking light) and 35 (earth = ground connection). The leads 10 (dipped beam light), 11 (long beam light), 16 (parking light), 17 (earth/ground) are connected to right-hand headlamp. Each headlamp contains a 12V/25/25 W Bilux lamp for long and dipped beam lights and 12V/2 W parking lamp.

5. The stop and license plate light is fixed in the center at rear on air intake unit above the license plate. It features two festoon-type bulbs: a 12V/15W lamp for the stop light and a 12V/3W lamp for illumination of license plate. From cable connector unit II/4 the lead 45 is taken to positive pole of stop light. The festoon bulb for license plate illumination has shunt connection and receives current from right-hand tail lamp via lead 44. The earth (ground) connection for all these lamps is also taken from the right-hand tail lamp.

6. The tail lamps are recessed in the corners of rear panel, just above the bumper. Each tail lamp unit contains a festoon-type bulb 12V/5W. From connector unit II/6 the lead 43 is taken to the positive terminal of right-hand tail lamp. The earth (ground) terminal is connected by lead 40 to cable connector unit II/7. From cable connector unit II/5 runs the lead 46 to the positive terminal of left-hand lamp, whereas the earth (ground) terminal is connected by lead 42 to earth lead 41 in stop and license plate light, to which it (lead 41) comes from the right-hand tail lamp.

7. The two directional signal lights are fixed to side panel, right and left, each of them being fitted with a 12V/15W festoon-type bulb. The left-hand lamp receives current via lead 7 and cable connector unit I/8 whereas the earth (ground) lead is connected by lead 14 to connector unit I/14. The right-hand lamp receives current via lead 6 and connector unit I/9. The earth terminal is connected by lead 15 to connector unit II/7.

8. The windscreen wiper motor is fitted to inner side of door at the right of instrument panel. The wiper motor's positive terminal is connected by lead 81 to fuse 6. The switch is located upon the wiper motor.

9. Except the connections in instrument panel all leads are arranged in several wiring assemblies as follows:

    a) Wiring assembly from instrument panel to cable connector unit I.

    b) Wiring assembly (central harness) links connector unit I with connector unit II and provides connection to right-hand headlamp and right-hand directional signal light.

c) Wiring assembly (left branch) links left-hand headlamp and horn with connector unit I.

d) Wiring assembly (rear branch) links cable connector unit II with the lamps on vehicle rear end.

e) Wiring assembly to steering column links the terminals of switches fitted to steering column guide with the corresponding instruments in the facia panel.

f) Wiring assembly from dynamo starter links cable connector unit II with dynamo starter and ignition coil.

10. Elastic connector bar. Two 7-pole connector bars, fitted in line on the left-hand front wheel housing, form the cable connector unit I. A 7-pole connector bar, inside the right-hand bottom corner of body rear panel, constitutes the cable connector unit II.

Note: The removal of the body requires disconnection of the following leads:

a) All leads linking cable connector unit II with dynamo starter and ignition coil. Remove the seat for this purpose.

b) The leads to the stop light switch.

c) The leads to electric horn.

Wiring diagram Isetta

BLK Blinker-Kontrolle
   Direction indictor control light

FLK Fernlicht-Kontrolle
   Headlamp control light

TB Tacho-Beleuchtung
   Speedometer light

LK Lade-Kontrolle
   Ignition control light

SK Schleifkonatakt
   Slide contact

SD Signaldrucker
   Horn button

Scheinwerfer rechts
   Headlamp (right)

Scheinwerfer links
   Headlamp (left)

Sicherungsdose
   Fuse box

Scheibenwischer
   Wiper motor

Horn
   Horn

ZundanlaB-Schalter
   Ignition and starter switch

Lichtschalter
   Lighting switch

Blinkgeber
> Directional flasher

Blinkerschalter
> Directional signal switch

Abblendschalter
> Headlamp dipper switch

Kabelverbind.-Klemme I
> Cable connector unit No. I

Blinkleuchte rechts
> Directional signal light (right)

Blinkleuchte links
> Directional signal light (left)

Kabelverbindungsklemme II
> Cable connector unit No. II

Batterie
> Battery

Bremslichtschalter
> Stop lamp switch

Reglerschalter
> Regulator & cut-out

Lichtanlasser
> Dynamo starter

Zundspule
> Ignition coil

Schlublicht rechts
> Tail light (right)

Schlublicht links
    Tail light (left)

Brems-Kennzeichenleuchte
    Stop & License plate light

Isetta Factory Repair Manual

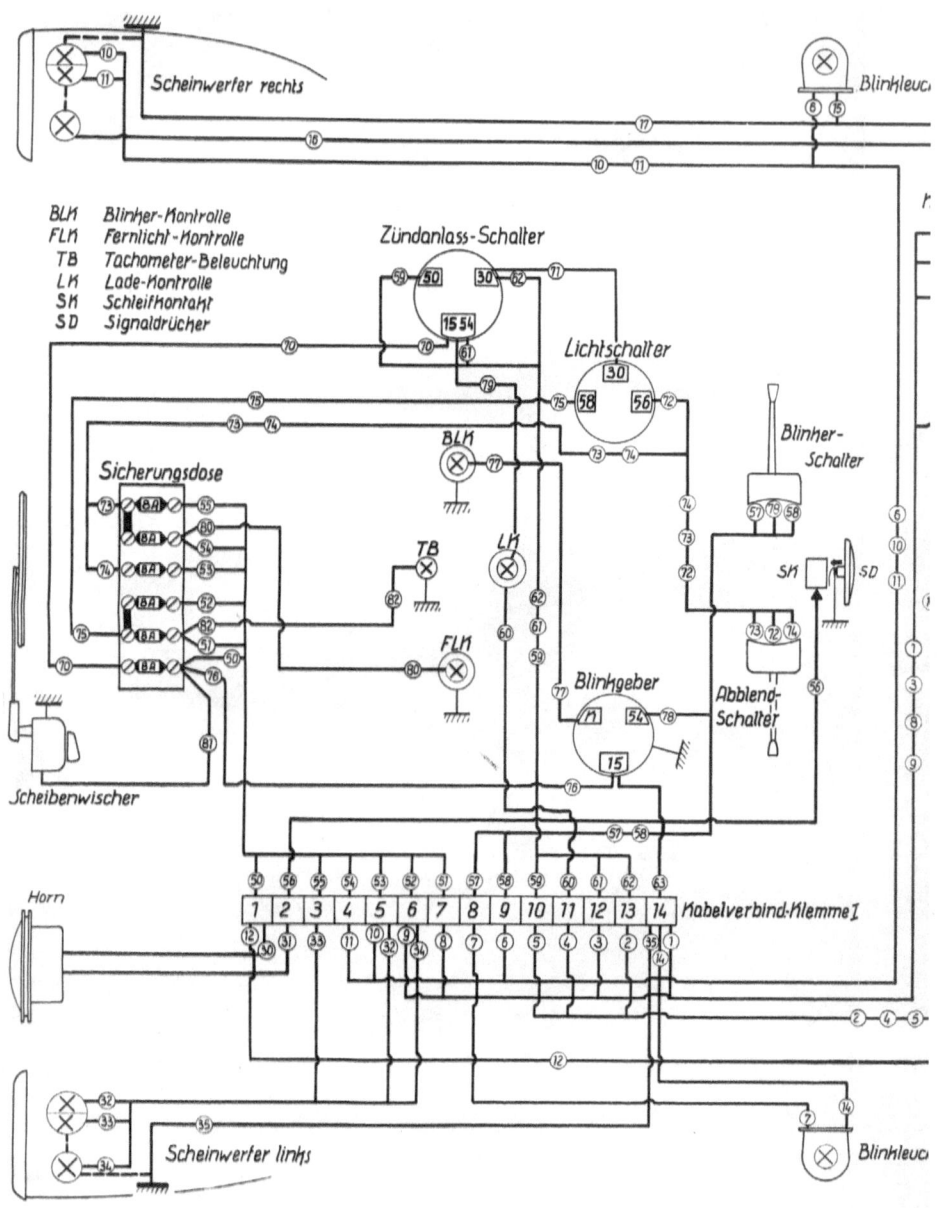

Isetta Factory Repair Manual

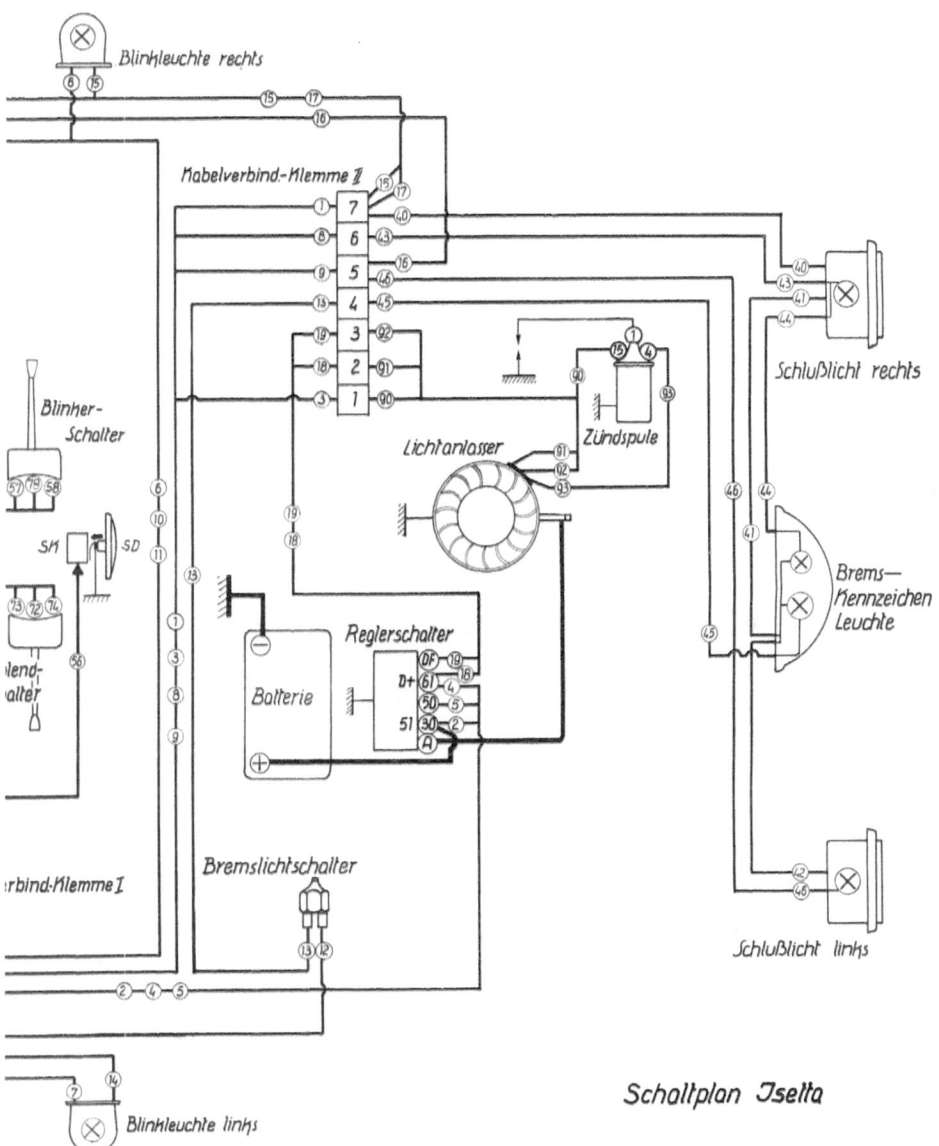

Schaltplan Isetta

E5 Replacing contact breaker points

Fig. 1

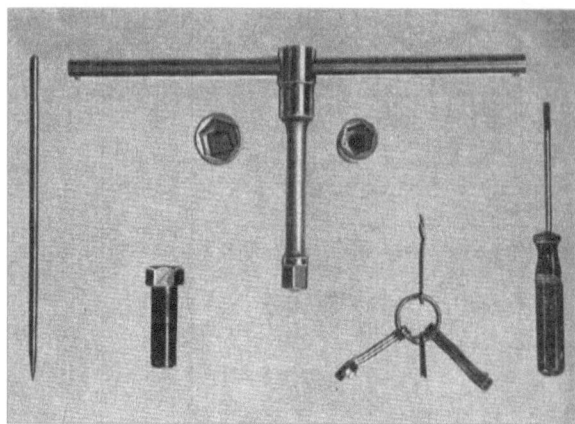

Tools: Screwdriver 6 mm, socket spanner 17/22 mm, puller screw for blower wheel No. 527, scriber, 1 set of contact spanners.

Fig. 2

1. Remove blower wheel housing. (screwdriver 6 mm)

2. Remove dynamo front end cap. (screwdriver 6 mm)

3. Unscrew blower wheel screw. (socket spanner 17 mm)

4. Remove blower wheel by means of puller screw No. 527. (puller screw No. 527, socket wrench 22 mm)

Isetta Factory Repair Manual

Fig. 3

5. Slacken screw securing contact breaker lead. (open ended spanner 5.5 mm)

Fig. 4

<u>Caution</u>: Spring for breaker arm is slotted, so that this screw must not be removed entirely.

6. Remove spring lock washer retaining the breaker arm. (scriber)

Fig. 5

<u>Caution</u>: Hold spring lock washer with the finger to avoid jumping away.

7. Remove breaker arm.

8. Detach contact support. (screwdriver 6 mm)

To fit the new breaker points proceed in exactly the reverse order.

Caution: Before fitting the breaker arm fill the bearing bushing with Bosch grease F t 1 v 22. Upon having fitted new breaker points it is indispensable to reset the ignition timing (see M 30 Figures 81-85).

E6 Replacing springs of automatic advance unit, and greasing the cam

Fig. 6

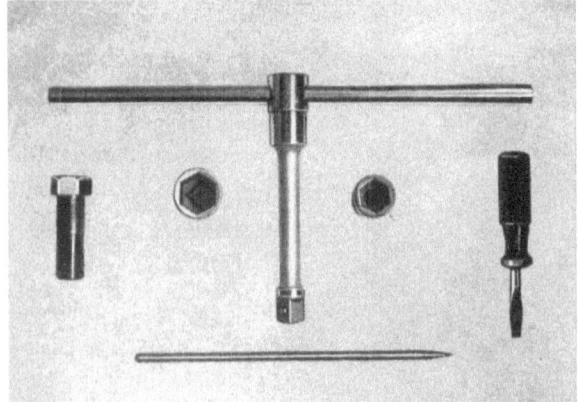

Tools: Screwdriver 6 mm, socket spanner 17/22 mm, puller screw for blower wheel No. 527, scriber.

Fig. 7

1. Remove blower wheel housing. (screwdriver 6 mm)

2. Remove dynamo front end cap. (screwdriver 6 mm)

3. Unscrew blower wheel fixing screw. (socket spanner 17 mm)

4. Remove blower wheel by means of puller screw. (puller screw No. 527, socket spanner)

5. Mark position of cam. (coloured pencil or brass scriber)

Fig. 8

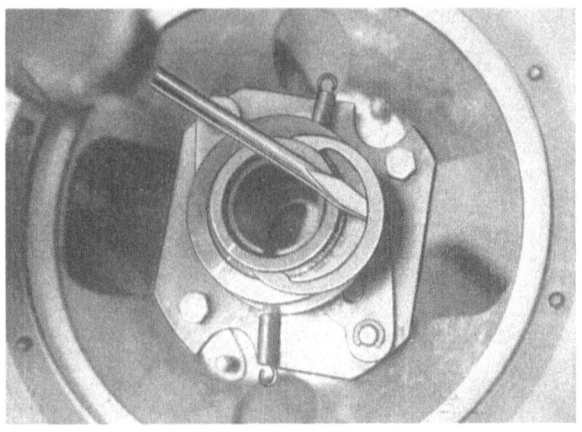

6. Unhook advance springs. (scriber)

7. Remove lock ring for breaker cam. (screwdriver)

Fig. 9

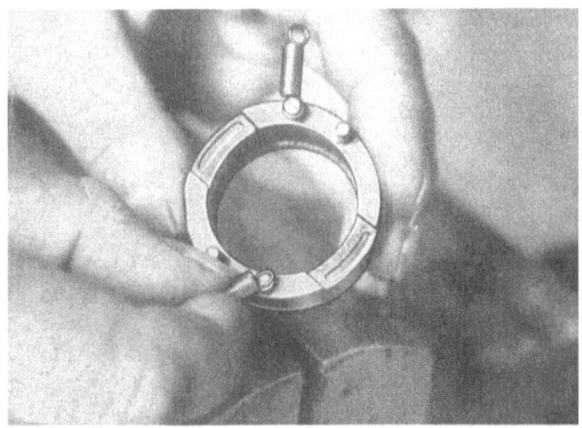

8. Unhook advance springs on breaker cam.

Caution: The advance springs are calibrated and must not be modified by extending them.

Fig. 10

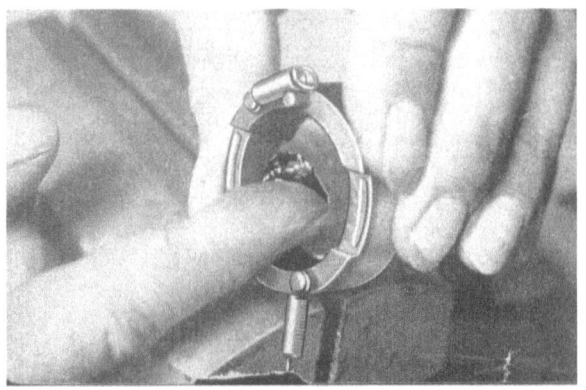

Caution: The breaker cam should be greased inside before being fitted. Fill groove machined in inner side of breaker cam with lubricating grease. The reassembly is carried out in exactly the reverse order. Fit the breaker cam into its original position, determined by the colour marks.

E7 Replacing carbon brushes

Fig. 11

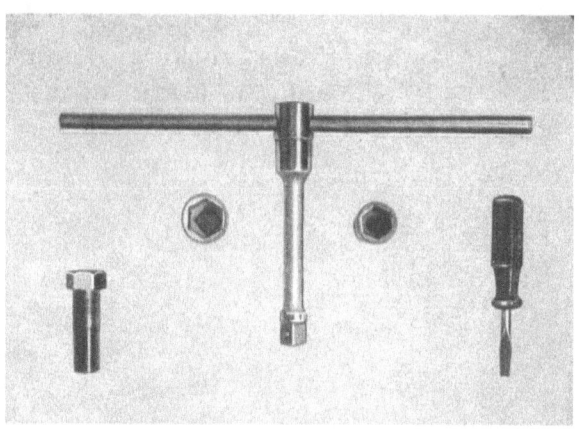

Tools: Screwdriver 6 mm, socket spanner 17/22 mm, puller screw for blower wheel No. 527.

Fig. 12

1. Remove blower wheel housing. (screwdriver 6 mm)

2. Remove dynamo front end cap. (screwdriver 6 mm)

3. Unscrew blower wheel fixing screw. (socket spanner 17 mm)

4. Remove blower wheel by means of puller screw. (puller screw No. 527, socket spanner)

5. Remove sheet-meal cover from dynamo (generator) housing. (screwdriver 6 mm)

Fig. 13

6. Withdraw brush springs from top of carbon brushes and release them laterally. (screwdriver)

Fig. 14

7. Slacken brush lead attaching screw. (screwdriver 6 mm)

Fig. 15

8. Lift off the carbon brushes and fit the new set.

Caution: Make certain positive and negative brush leads are not too close to each other.

The reassembly is carried out in exactly the reverse order.

E9 Testing carbon brushes for circuit and ground (earth)

Fig. 16

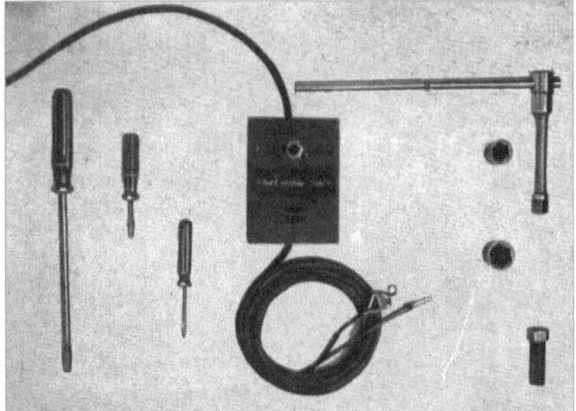

Tools: Screwdriver 6/8 mm, electric screwdriver, socket spanner 17/22 mm, puller screw for blower wheel No. 527, test lamp.

Fig. 17

1. Remove blower wheel housing. (screwdriver 6 mm)

2. Remove dynamo front end cap. (screwdriver 6 mm)

3. Unscrew blower wheel fixing screw. (socket spanner 17 mm)

4. Remove blower wheel by means of puller screw. (puller screw No. 527, socket spanner)

5. Remove sheet-meal cover from dynamo (generator) housing. (screwdriver 6 mm)

6. Lift off all springs from carbon brushes, withdraw the brushes. (screwdriver)

7. Disconnect leads 15 and 1 from ignition coil.

8. Disconnect battery lead from starter connection. (screwdriver)

9. Disconnect leads green, blue and black/red from cable connector unit in the vehicle and

draw them out. (see Group A1 Figure 4) (electric screwdriver)

10. Detach dynamo (generator) housing. (screwdriver 8 mm)

Fig. 18

Caution: When testing hold in mind that 2 brush holders have ground (earth) connection, 2 brush holders are insulated.

11. Disconnect positive connections from the two insulated brush holders. (screwdriver 6 mm)

Fig. 19

12. Test the grounded (earthed) brush holders (negative), by connecting one test lamp probe to the housing and the other probe to the brush holder. The test lamp must light.

Fig. 20

13. Test the insulated brush holders (positive), by connecting one test lamp probe to the housing and the other probe to the brush holder. The test lamp must not light.

The reassembly is carried out in exactly the reverse order.

E10 Testing field coils for circuit and ground (earth)

Tools: Same set as for E9. Screwdriver 6/8 mm, electric screwdriver, socket spanner 17/22 mm, puller screw for blower wheel No. 527, test lamp.

For steps 1 to 10 see sections E7 and E9 for associated pictures.

1. Remove blower wheel housing. (screwdriver 6 mm)

2. Remove dynamo front end cap. (screwdriver 6 mm)

3. Unscrew blower wheel fixing screw. (socket spanner 17 mm)

4. Remove blower wheel by means of puller screw. (puller screw No. 527, socket spanner)

5. Remove sheet-meal cover from dynamo (generator) housing. (screwdriver 6 mm)

6. Lift off all springs from carbon brushes, withdraw the brushes. (screwdriver)

7. Disconnect leads 15 and 1 from ignition coil.

8. Disconnect battery lead from starter connection. (screwdriver)

9. Disconnect leads green, blue and black/red from cable connector unit in the vehicle and draw them out. (see Group A1 Figure 4) (electric screwdriver)

10. Detach dynamo (generator) housing. (screwdriver 8 mm)

Fig. 21

11. Disconnect field coil leads from brush holders.

12. Test starter field coils for circuit by connecting one test lamp probe to the field coil terminal lead and the other probe to starter lead terminal stud. The test lamp must light.

Fig. 22

13. Test starter field coils for ground (earth) by connecting one test lamp probe to starter lead terminal stud and the other probe to the dynamo cover. The test lamp must not light.

Fig. 23

14. Test dynamo (generator) field coils for circuit by connecting one test lamp probe to field coil terminal lead and the other probe to brush lead of field coil. The test lamp must light.

Fig. 24

15. Test dynamo (generator) field coils for ground by connecting one test lamp probe to field coil terminal lead and the other probe to the dynamo cover plate. The test lamp must not light.

Fig. 25

16. Test field coils of starter and dynamo for mutual ground by connecting one test lamp probe to terminal lead of starter coil and the other probe to brush lead of dynamo coil. The test lamp must not light.

E12 Testing armature of Dynamo starter

Fig. 26

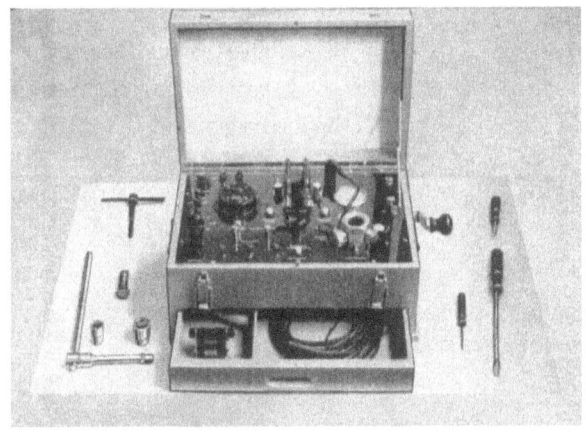

Tools: Screwdriver 6/8 mm, socket spanner 17/22 mm, puller screw for blower wheel No. 527, puller spindle for armature of dynamo starter No. 528, testing equipment Prufrex for electric sets (item shown in figure is type K15).

For steps 1 to 6 see section E9 for the relevant diagrams.

1. Remove blower wheel housing. (screwdriver 6 mm)

2. Remove dynamo front end cap. (screwdriver 6 mm)

3. Unscrew blower wheel fixing screw. (socket spanner 17 mm)

4. Remove blower wheel by means of puller screw. (puller screw No. 527, socket spanner)

5. Remove sheet-meal cover from dynamo (generator) housing. (screwdriver 6 mm)

6. Lift off all springs from carbon brushes, withdraw the brushes. (screwdriver)

Fig. 27

7. Detach dynamo housing. (screwdriver 8 mm)

8. Remove dynamo housing. (with the aid of 2 screwdrivers applied behind the flange of dynamo housing).

9. Remove armature from crankshaft extension by means of puller spindle No. 528.

Fig. 28

10. Locate armature assembly upon the testing equipment. (Prufrex K15)

a) Place detector magnet upon laminated iron core, switch on the equipment and rotate armature slowly.

Fig. 29

A defective armature wiring is indicated by the glowing of an incandescent glass tube on the testing equipment (shortened armature).

b) Short-circuit the commutator by surrounding it with a wire. Check laminated iron core with the detector magnet by turning armature slowly.

Fig. 30

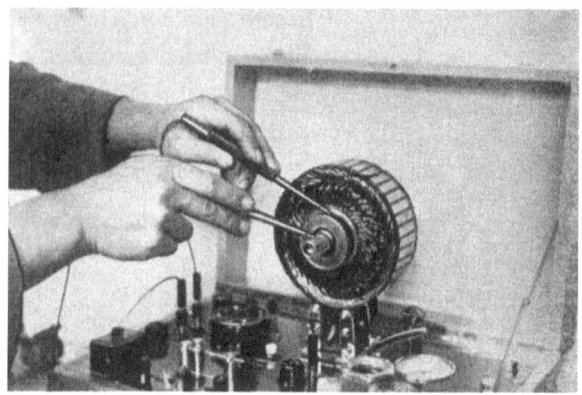

If there is a break in the wiring the incandescent glass tube does not light.

c) Check commutator bars and armature core (shaft) with the aid of test points.

A grounded armature is indicated by a humming noise produced by the testing equipment. (grounded armature)

E13 Testing ignition coil

Tools: Socket spanner 10 mm, open ended spanner 9 mm, Prufrex testing equipment.

Fig. 31

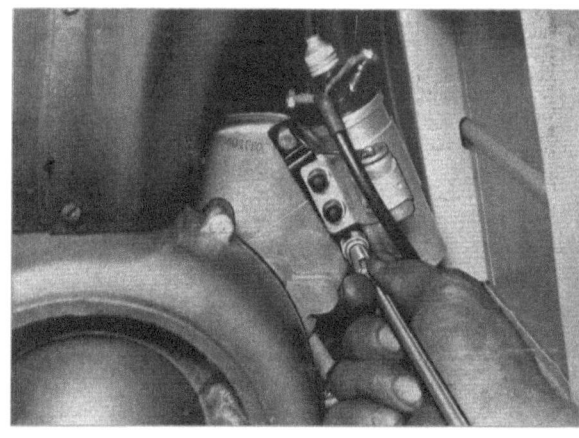

1. Remove high-tension lead from ignition coil.

2. Detach connections 1 and 15 from the ignition coil. (open ended spanner 9 mm)

3. Detach ignition coil with holding bracket. (socket spanner 10 mm)

Fig. 32

4. Locate ignition coil upon the testing equipment and check it by means of spark discharge over the provided gap.

E15 Testing condenser

Tools: Screwdriver 6 mm, open ended spanner 9 mm.

Fig. 33

1. Detach connection to ignition coil. (open ended spanner 9 mm)

2. Detach condenser from holding clip on ignition coil. (screwdriver)

Fig. 34

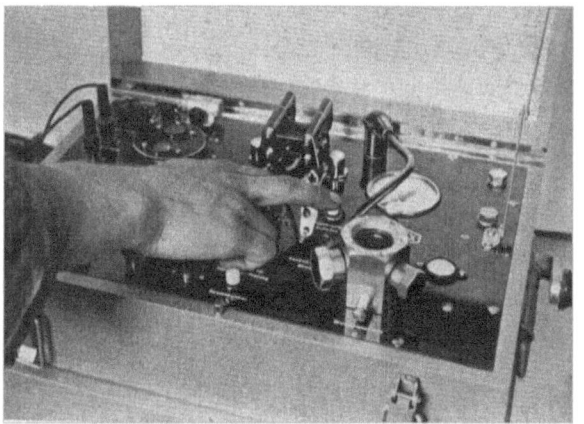

3. Fit condenser upon testing equipment and switch on the tester set.

4. Charge condenser.

Fig. 35

5. Discharge condenser.

E17 Aiming the headlamps

Fig. 36

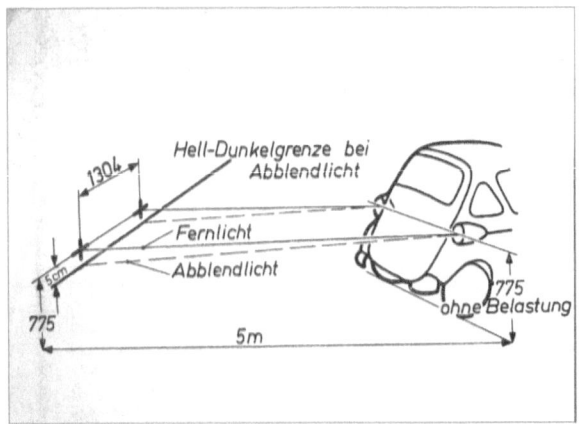

Tools: Screwdriver 6 mm, aiming screen or aiming device.

Fig. 37

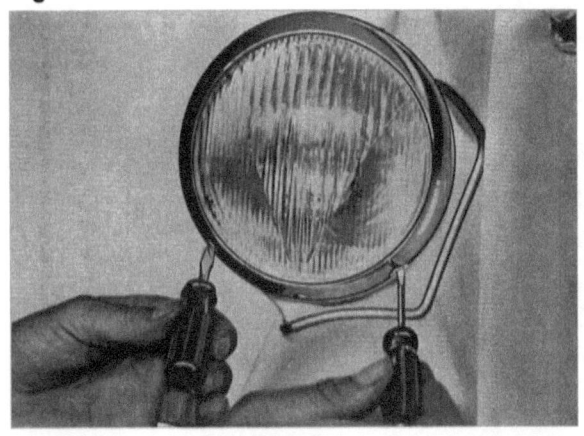

1. Vertical adjustment up and down is done by uniform motion of the two adjusting screws. Turning them inwards raises the headlamp, and unscrewing lowers the beam.

Fig. 38

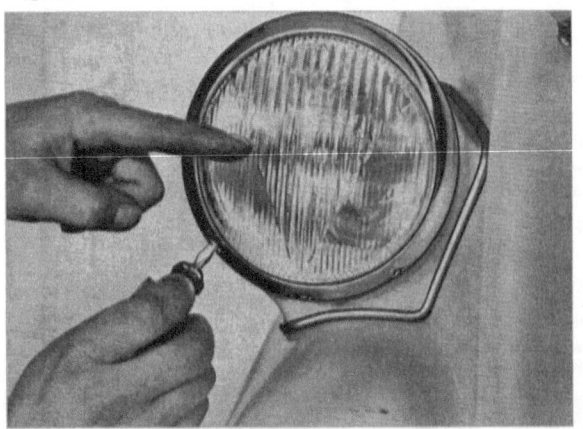

2. For horizontal adjustment to the right and the left it is mostly sufficient to turn one screw in or outwards as required, whereas for a wide adjustment range it is necessary to turn both screws in opposite direction. Having done the horizontal adjustment correct the vertical position.

Isetta Factory Repair Manual

E19 Replacing a Bilux lamp

Fig. 39

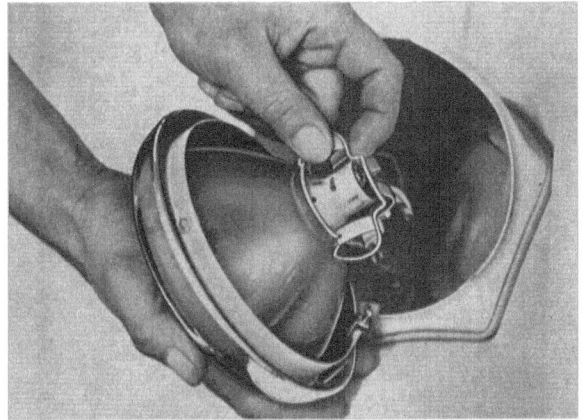

Tools: Screwdriver 6 mm.

1. Loosen the headlamp by removing the screw in center of bottom and tilt headlamp upwards.

2. Remove retaining clip for lamp holder.

Fig. 40

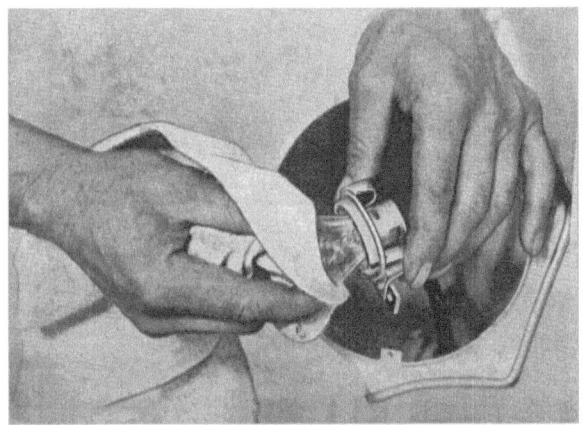

3. Turn lamp out of socket.

Caution: A Bilux lamp should only be touched with a clean cloth or paper, as otherwise the sweat and oil on the hand might dim the reflector.

www.VelocePress.com

GROUP W
MAINTENANCE

Jobs to be performed

The numerals correspond with the lubrication point indications and the illustrations of the lubricator chart.

1. Pedal shaft	Lubricating grease
2. Universal joint, steering	Lubricating grease
3. Steering arm shaft	Lubricating grease
4. King pins, right and left	Lubricating grease
5. Wheel bearings, right and left	Lubricating grease
6. Swing arm shafts, right and left	Lubricating grease
7. Brake master cylinder	ATE brake fluid blue
8. Battery	Distilled water
9. Contact breaker	High-temperature bearing grease
10. Engine	Engine oil
11. Rear suspension leaf spring	Caramba (Chassis spray oil)
12. Rear drive	Transmission oil
13. Air cleaner	Blow through
14. Transmission	Transmission oil

Legend of symbols used for lubricants and maintenance products

Engine oil	Summer SAE 40
	Winter SAE 20
Transmission oil (O level check)	SAE 40
Lubricating grease	
Distilled water	
Brake Fluid	ATE blue
Caramba (Chassis spray oil)	
High-temperature bearing grease	

Isetta Factory Repair Manual

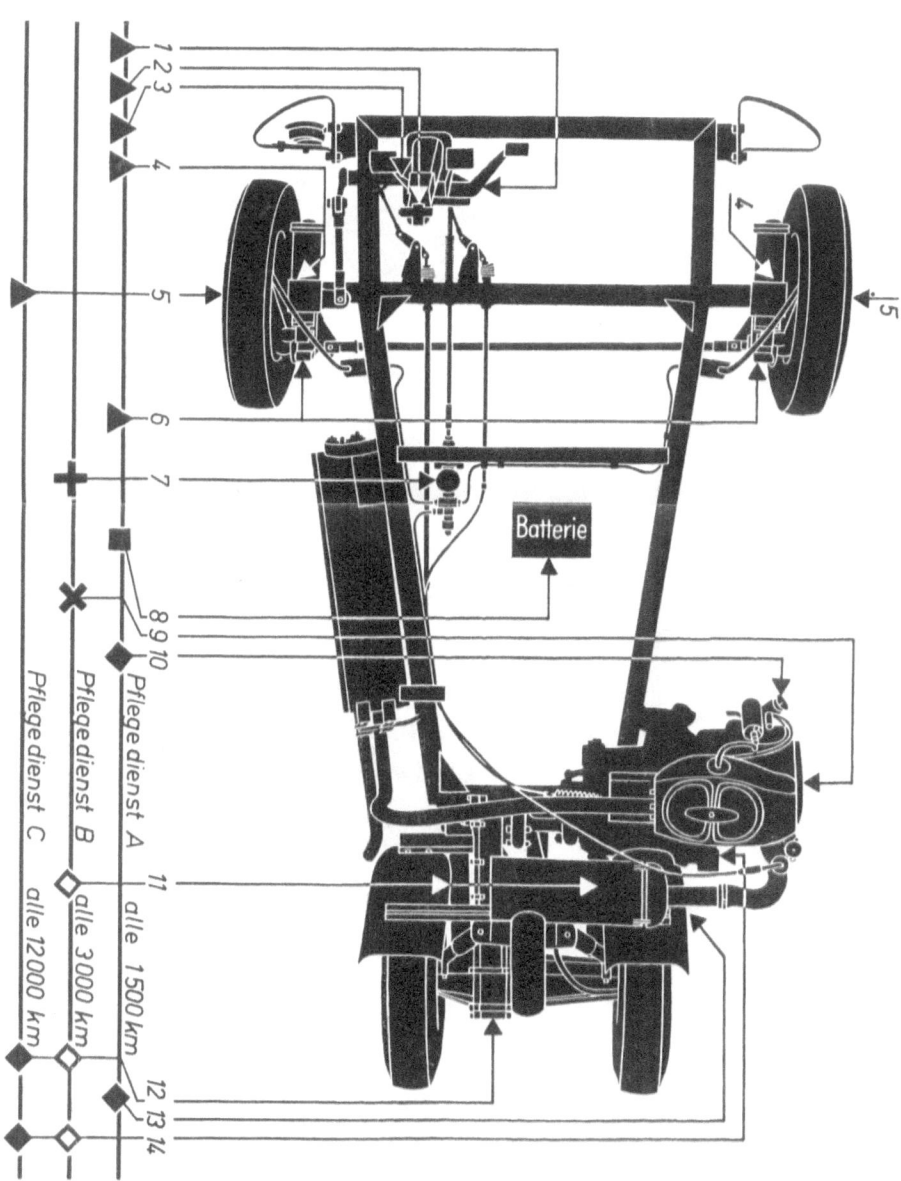

Isetta Factory Repair Manual

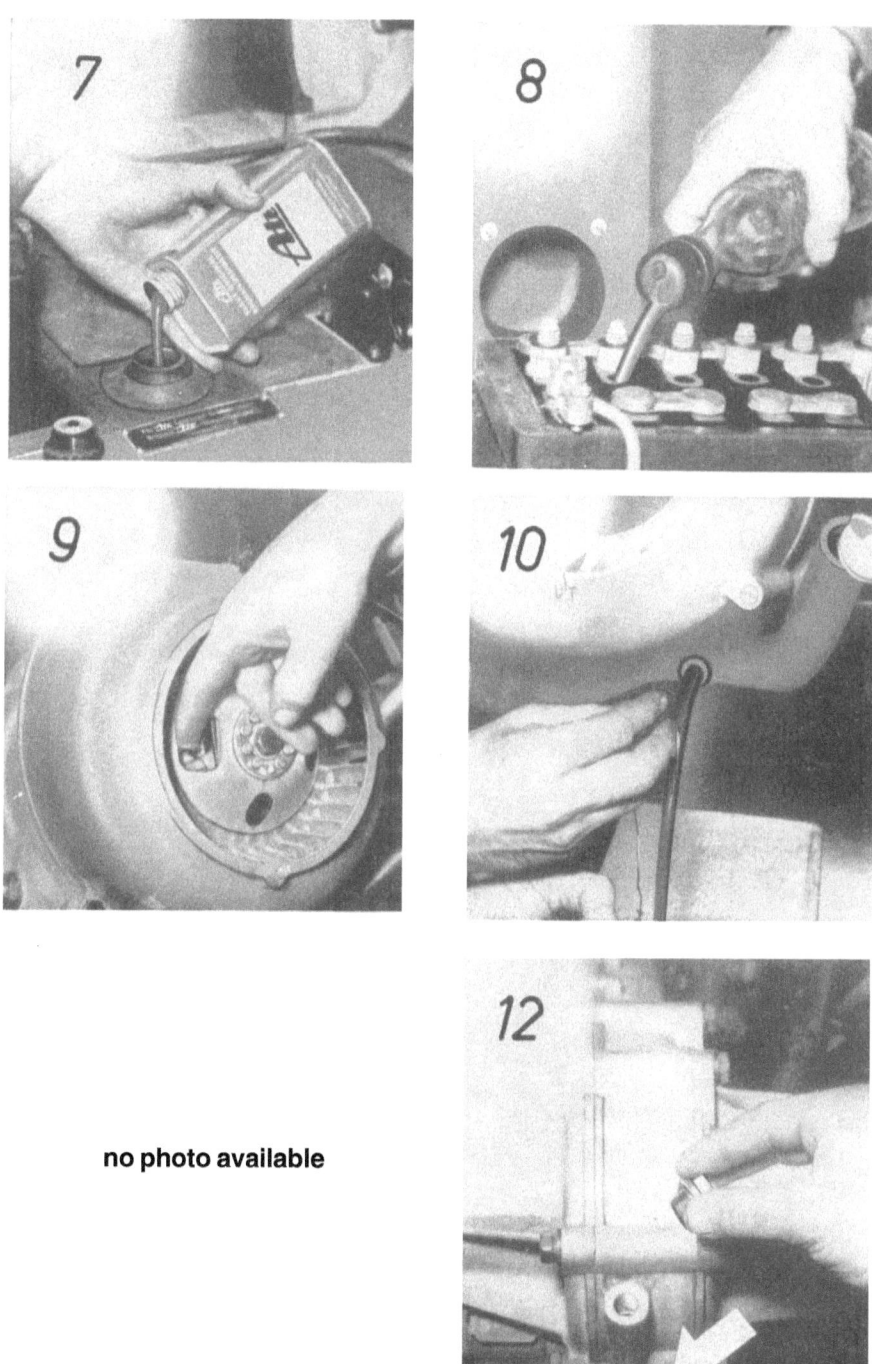

no photo available

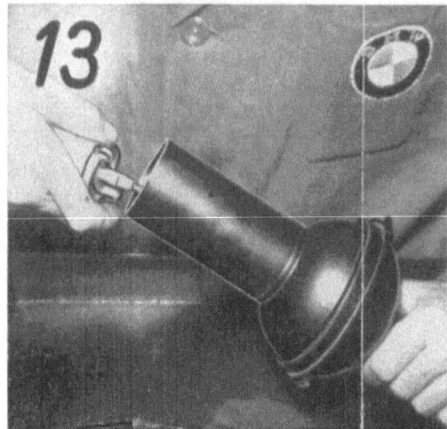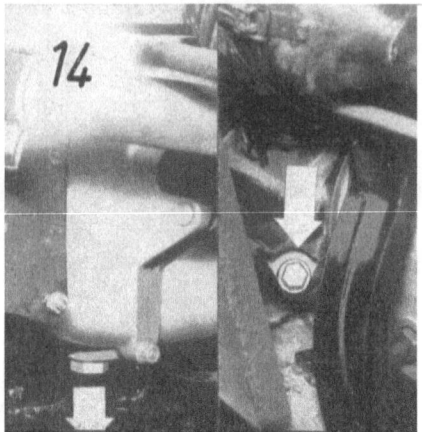

www.ingramcontent.com/pod-product-compliance
Lightning Source LLC
Chambersburg PA
CBHW020124240426
43673CB00038B/589